Helen S. Law.

GW00647599

from Maud.
December '84.

CANEWORK

THE BASKET-MAKER'S RHYME

I can rand,
At your command,
  Put on a decent border;
Upset tight,
Wale all right,
  And keep my stakes in order.

CANEWORK

CHARLES CRAMPTON

including an
Introduction to the History of Basket-making
and some notes on Cane and its uses

DRYAD PRESS LTD

LONDON

© Dryad Press Ltd, 1984
24th Edition

All rights reserved. No part of this publication
may be reproduced, in any form or by any means,
without permission from the Publisher

ISBN 0852 1 9131 6

Printed in Great Britain by
Butler & Tanner Ltd
Frome, Somerset
for the publishers
Dryad Press Ltd
4 Fitzhardinge Street
London W1H 0AH

CONTENTS

PREFACE

This book has long been regarded as a standard work, and its success is undoubtedly due to the sound principles and practical nature of the text, resulting from the author's long workshop experience. We know of no other book written by one who has been 'on the plank', as it is termed in the trade, with the exception of Crampton's own *Junior Basket Maker*, A. G. Knock's *Willow Basketwork* (both published by the Dryad Press), and the late Mr. Okey's *Willow Work*.

Charles Crampton came from a basket-making family. To his years of trade experience he added a considerable amount of teaching, his object being to explain the elements of basketry in a simple way through the making of a series of articles suitable for everyday use.

While the best place to learn a craft is undoubtedly the workshop where people earn their living by it, such facilities are not always available, and from the instructions given here any amateur should be able to make good progress and extend his knowledge. Those who wish to teach the craft to others have, of course, a special responsibility to acquire the proper technique. If unable to work under a qualified basket-maker, they would do well to supplement their study and practice by a visual aid.

At the end of this book, the teacher will find further assistance in the form of an outline scheme for a four-year course in cane basketry, accompanied by schedules of the materials and tools required for classes of different age groups.

All the articles described are made with what is known as pulp cane (that is, the cut centre of cane), as it is the most easily handled material for the amateur, being pliable to work when damp and obtainable in long lengths. Willow, though a beautiful material, is difficult to work and consequently less widely used in schools.

Cane, like all natural products, varies considerably in quality, and the beginner should beware of low-priced and inferior material which will hinder his efforts, waste his time, and result in articles poor in shape and rough at every bend. The real craftsman prefers to select his cane irrespective of price, because it not only saves time but produces a superior article. The reader can do no better than follow his example and constantly bear in mind the motto of all fine craftsmen,

'You cannot do good work with poor materials'

CHAPTER I

AN INTRODUCTION TO THE HISTORY OF BASKET-MAKING

Fig. 1. AN APACHE WATER JAR OF
DIAGONAL TWINED WEAVING
COVERED WITH PITCH

Fig. 1 A
A PRIMITIVE MOHAVE BASKET

Basket-making was one of the first crafts, and its uses to primitive man have been well illustrated by the researches among the American Indians of Mr. Otis Mason and G. Wharton James, whose books are the best introduction for those who wish to study the history of the craft.

The materials were to hand in all countries—willow, split wood, rush, roots, bark and grasses were used in the colder countries; cane, bamboo, palm leaf and fibres in the warmer. All these could be prepared with the aid of teeth and hands, and cut with sharp stones or shells, basket-making beyond this only requiring a pointed bone for a bodkin.

Thus we find nearly everything from the cradle to the grave made of basket-work. The hut or shelter, the trap to catch game, the boat or coracle, the storage basket. Water was heated in clay-covered baskets by placing hot stones in the water; it was carried in clay- or pitch-covered jars, and finally, among the American Indians, a basket was put into the grave, containing things required for the next world. There is much in common between the basket-making instinct and the nest-building of birds, and perhaps the most primitive basket known is the grain basket of the Mohave Indians of North America, about which Mr. Otis Mason tells us in his book on Indian Basketry, and which appears to be made much as a bird puts its nest together. This basket is from 3 ft. to 5 ft. across and 2 ft. to 3 ft. deep, and stands on a platform made for it with long poles, and when full of grain is domed with mud to carry off the rain.

The oldest basket-work that has come down to us is the coiled, or as we term it, Indian work, which is common to many races, and most beautiful examples are still being produced by some primitive people in America and Africa today.

Among the American Indians basket-making was a woman's art, and so important was it to them that it has been woven into all their early legends.

There is a story of how the two first baby baskets were made. The Gods of War were born of two women. One had the sun for father, the other had the waterfall, and when they were born they were placed in baby baskets both alike. They had footrests and back battens made of the sunbeam, hoods of rainbow, side strings of sheet lightning, and lacing strings of zigzag lightning. One child they covered with a black cloud and the other with rain.

All kinds of Indian ceremonial were bound up with basket-making, symbols being woven upon them for the various uses. Invalids had their elaborate performances to the healing goddesses. The dead were buried with baskets, and the Indian women saved their finest productions against their burial.

The Indian girl made baskets for her future home, and her value was enhanced if she was a good basket-maker. She would weave into them the doings of her lover, his hunting, etc.

There were basket dances, basket throwing, and many other ceremonies, some of which are still carried on in Mexico and in the United States among the Indians.

The variety of materials used by the Indians adds, of course, to the interests of their baskets and affects their colour and pattern. All kinds of grasses, palm leaves, corn leaves, rushes, hemp, aloe, yucca, willow, roots of cedar, spruce, alder, etc., are made use of. The colours for dyeing are mainly brown, red,

Fig. 2. NORTH AMERICAN INDIAN BASKETRY

Probably Pima basket, Gulf of California.   Linen basket: the break in the pattern is
to allow the spirit to enter.

From T. A. Joyce's Collection, with permission

Fig. 3. EXAMPLES OF EGYPTIAN BASKET-WORK

18th Dynasty, Middle Empire (*c.* 1400 B.C.)

1, 2 and 3. Sandals of palm leaf.   4 and 5. Examples of coiled basket-work.
6. Coiled mat (? rush).

black, and yellow, though others are used, and all are got from roots, barks, etc. The yucca is said to be a great favourite, giving red from its roots and yellow from its leaves. The Indians, too, have a colour symbolism, which varies slightly with the tribe, like weaves and patterns. Generally red is a sacred colour associated with the East and success, blue with the North, standing for defeat and trouble, black with the West and death, and white for peace and happiness.

Of pattern there is practically no end—sun, moon, stars, animals, plants, clouds, trees, dances, weapons, ripples in the lake, birds flying, etc.

Indian or coiled basket-work can be seen in most ethnographical collections from all parts of the world today, and the primitive man, making himself a useful basket with a little play in the pattern, often puts us to shame by the beautiful thing he produces. The Egyptian has left us traces of many varieties of basket-work, including the use of plaited and coiled work, especially for household utensils. It is interesting to note that coiled baskets are made today by certain peoples in both Central and parts of West Africa very similar in shape and colour. It was used for furniture and the seating of chairs and for elaborate sandal work in great variety. Examples up to 3000 B.C. are to be seen in museums.

Sir William Flinders Petrie found quantities of fine coiled and other basket-work on his Egyptian excavations, and the designs and shape of the earliest pots found in Egypt suggest that they were copied from basket-work. The Pitt Rivers Museum at Oxford has examples of Egyptian and native basket-work in great varieties. In the Bible story concerning Joseph, you will remember when he interpreted the chief baker's dream, how the latter says, 'and, behold, I had three white baskets on my head, and in the uppermost basket there was of all manner of bakemeats for Pharaoh; and the birds did eat them out of the basket upon my head'. Coiled baskets of this sort are used in Egypt and Palestine to this day and carried on the head.

Sir Leonard Woolley found impressions of coiled basket-work on pottery at Ur in Mesopotamia, dating from about 3000 B.C. Herodotus, in the fifth century B.C., tells of basket boats covered with bitumen being used on the Euphrates, and such boats are

Fig. 4. CORACLES AFLOAT. FOR NETTING SALMON

Fig. 5. ANCIENT POTTERY SHOWING BASKET-WORK IMPRESSIONS

(*Left*) Impression of slath bottom of basket on base of pot from Phylakopi, Melos. Date *c*.2500 B.C.

(*Right*) Impression of rush mat on which the pot was formed. From Amorgos: Bronze age.

Examples in Ashmolean Museum, Oxford. Reproduced by permission

still used there today, also in India. The skin-covered coracle of our forefathers can still be seen on the Severn.

It seems probable that the peoples of Northern Europe made a type of basket-work starting with the slath base and not coiled work, owing to the use of willow. The slath does not seem to occur in ancient Egyptian work. The furthest south where examples have been found of this till after Roman times, is in the Greek island of Melos, where a piece of pottery has been found made by a Northern race, on which the impression of the slath is to be seen. An example is in the Taylorian Museum in Oxford, the date being about 2500 B.C. They also have a piece with the impression of a rush basket, suggesting in both cases that the basket was used as a mould for the pottery.

Baskets were connected with both Greek and Roman religious life, where they were the receptacle for the offerings to the gods. Likewise in Christian times we find a symbol of the eucharist— the loaves and fishes—includes a basket as a receptacle.

The Romans made furniture of wicker, and Pliny tells us that they and the Etruscans reclined upon couches of willow.

The example of a Roman wicker chair given in Fig. 6 is from a tombstone in the Trèves Museum, and the type of gravestone can be seen repeated in coarser workmanship in the Mainz Museum.

The English tradition in basket-work is inherited from the Celts, and Fig. 7 shows a very early British example of what was probably a wattle wall. Several Roman writers refer to the prevalence of this method of hut building in Great Britain.

It is possible that the excellent willows grown in northern Europe influenced the type of basket made, just as one finds in Norway and Sweden the split wood basket, which still exists in the Lake District and at Bewdley. The swills, as they are called in the Lakes, are made of split oak with hazel rims, and the names for the various parts suggest that it may be a Norse survival.

In Surrey there still exists the trug or split ash basket.

Lobster pots, or baskets for catching lobsters, are still made in the Isle of Wight and elsewhere, and eel traps made of willow are still used in France. They were used till quite recently in Oxfordshire and the Fen district, where they were called eel grigs. There is an example in the excellent Bygones Collection

Fig. 6. ROMAN WICKER CHAIR, *c.* A.D. 200, TRÈVES

Fig. 7. SPECIMEN OF BASKET-WORK FOUND IN GLASTONBURY LAKE VILLAGE EXCAVATIONS; EARLY IRON AGE

By kind permission of Dr. A. Bulleid, F.S.A. and Mr. H. St. George Gray, F.S.A.

at the Peterborough Museum, along with other specimens of basket-work.

Another curious use of basket-work, which lapsed about seventy-five years ago, was the making of bug traps to put under pillows. The baskets were shaken out in the morning and insects destroyed. They were made in France until quite recently.

No one has yet made a collection of types of wicker cradle, which are now fast going out of use. There are several very fine old examples in the Amsterdam Museum.

Many kinds of traditional basket-work still exist at home and abroad, and are worth recording, especially the names used. For instance, Maund, from which we get the word Maundy Thursday, is still used in out-of-the-way places—a 'Riving Maund' for a fish basket; Cype or whisket, the Shropshire names for swill, previously referred to as made in the Lakes; groins made to preserve the foreshore are made of hazel woven by a method called 'Radling' in Barrow-in-Furness, possibly a variety of the word Randing.

Every district of Middle and Southern Europe has its back basket: French *Hotte*, German *Kiepen*, Italian *Gerlo*. These vary in shape and material, using willow, hazel, chestnut, etc.

There still exists a Basketmakers' Guild or Company among the ancient fraternities of the City of London. It was established in the year 1569, but unfortunately most of its old records were burnt in the Great Fire. In Queen Elizabeth's time the trade was largely carried on by foreigners, though there were in the Company's Ordinances various enactments to reduce their numbers and encourage English apprentices. In the year 1937 a Royal Charter was granted to the Basketmakers' Company by the late King George VI and later in the same year Queen Mary, who was keenly interested in British handicrafts, graciously accepted the Honorary Membership of the Company.

'The Warden of the Guild had powers conferred on him to search, view and oversee all manner of baskets, flaskets, scryns, maunds, and all other wares and stuff, and to denounce all such as they found unlawful, not well and workmanlike and strongly made, and wrought with good and reasonable stuff, and bring them to the Chamber of the City to be forfeited.'

Such were the good old days. This work was, of course, all

Fig. 8. BACK BASKETS

1. Lichtenfels, Germany	2. Crana, Italy	3. Dieppe, France
4. Berne, Switzerland	5. Piora, Switzerland	6. Valais, Switzerland
7. Goslar, Germany	8. Sarawak	9. Valais, Switzerland

B

Fig. 9. ENGLISH BASKET-WORK

1. Willow Southport basket. Made on a frame.
1a. Showing randed base of same.
2. Cane basket (Palembang).
2a. Base of same, illustrating slath foundation.
3. Scuttle made of natural and white willow.

3a. Showing ash slath base.
4. Potato basket, Monmouthshire. White willow on hazel frame.
5. Fish basket, Newcastle. Cane on hazel frame.
6. Oak swill, Lake District. Made on hazel frame with split oak strips (tars).

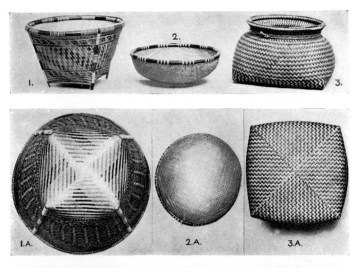

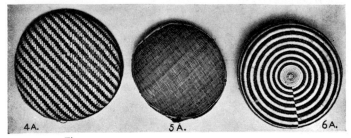

Fig. 10. AFRICAN AND EASTERN BASKETS

1. Round basket, square base, Sarawak. Typical Eastern type in black, red, and natural glossy cane. 1a. Base of this type.
2. Dyak basket of Bumban reed, Sarawak. 2a. Shows sieve or mesh weaving of same.
3. Basket on squared base, round top, dyed red and natural cane. Malay States, Kelantan.

3a. Base of same, diagonal weaving.
4. Basket treated with pitch as water scoop. Nyasa. 4a. Base of same.
5. Round basket, coarse weaving of split bamboo and cane. Zanzibar. 5a. Base of same.
6. Coiled raffia basket, yellow and black raffia on grass core. Sierra Leone. Typical West African basketwork. 6a. Base of same.

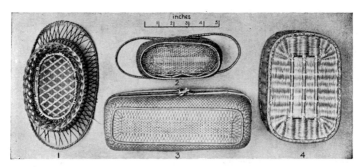

Fig. 11. EXAMPLES OF FINE OLD ENGLISH AND FRENCH
WILLOW SKEIN WORK
1. Small trinket basket.   2. Key basket.   3. Small French knitting basket.
4. English work basket in flat skein work.
Photographs show bases only, to illustrate different types of foundation.

wicker (willow). Such wardens would have a lot to condemn today. The late Mr. H. H. Bobart, a former Clerk to the Guild, published an interesting record of the Guild in his *Records of the Basketmakers' Company.*

English basketry, prior to the introduction of cane in recent times, was almost entirely willow, the natural native-grown material, though before 1914 a large part of our willow work was done with Belgian, French, German, and Madeira willows, because we would not grow enough of these in this country. The growth of the English willow is carried on in Somerset, the Thames Valley, Trent Valley and other districts, and its quality when properly grown is unequalled. So far as workmanship goes some of our hamper makers and willow basket-makers are hard to beat if given the chance, but the low wages paid for homework abroad has killed much of the finer work.

Lichtenfels, in Bavaria, is the centre of German basket-making, and at its basket school there is a small museum of baskets. There is another in Vienna.

The use of cane and bamboo in the East has led to other types of basket-work, especially in China, Japan, Malaya, and Borneo. Most Japanese work is made of split bamboo and it was usual to split up old bamboos used as house poles and coloured with smoke and age, to make fine baskets. Now it is stained to imitate old work, as we foolishly stain oak for sham Jacobean furniture.

Fine Japanese baskets are as wonderful in variety of weaving as they are beautiful in shape, but commercialism is ruining the good work, and each year competition brings worse copies of the traditional shapes, and the finer work gets rarer. Beautiful specimens can often be seen in museums.

Bamboo is a wonderful material, and the Chinese as well as the Japanese turn it to good account for baskets, etc. The old Chinese bamboo furniture was wonderful in workmanship and fine in design. They never used a nail in old bamboo work, pegs of the bamboo always being used.

Another very important material is the palm leaf, of which many kinds are used, including the Raffia palm, Buris palm, and the so-called Screw palm (Pandanus). The latter splits easily into any width and is the material used mostly in the East Indies. Palm leaf basketry is so extensive that it needs a special study of its own.

The authorities at Kew give *Borassus flatellifera* as one of the common palms for basket-work.

This little introduction to the story of basket-making may suggest lines of research into this much neglected subject.

The late Mr. Bobart, a former Clerk to the Basketmakers' Company, to whom reference has already been made, is the author of an excellent book—*Basketwork Through the Ages*, particulars of which are given in the Bibliography on page 27.

CHAPTER II

SOME NOTES ON CANE AND ITS USES

Rattan, or cane palms, are climbing plants which trail along the ground or climb the trees in the jungle and swamps of tropical countries. The best canes come from Malaysia and Indonesia. They belong to the genera *Calamus*, *Daemonorops*, etc., and grow to the great length of 200 to 600 ft.; an example at Kew measured

Fig. 12. THE RATTAN OR CANE (CALAMUS ROTANG)
A CREEPING PALM GROWING IN THE BOTANICAL GARDENS
AT BUITENSORG, DUTCH INDIES

584 ft. The average diameter is under 1 in., and rarely gets beyond 1½ in. The leaves are only found at the end of the shoots. The plants are erect when small and remain so until they attain the height of several feet, after which the stem needs support, which it receives from the aid of a long feeler or flagellum armed with hooked thorns, by means of which it clings to the vegetation.

The outer bark or sheath is also covered with thorns, and these extend along the underside of the centre stem of the leaf, from which projects the feeler or flagellum to a length of 18 in. beyond the leaf's tip. These thorns, or hooked spikes, are very strong and

Fig. 13. RATTAN LEAF SHOWING FLAGELLUM AND STEM

sharp, and make gathering of the cane difficult, the natives at
times refusing to work at this when there is easier work like
rubber collecting to be done. The pulp containing the seeds of
certain canes is eaten by the natives, and from the scales in the seed
of the *Daemonorops* species is made the Dragon's Blood of com-
merce, a sort of red resin used for colouring varnishes.

Cane is rarely cultivated and usually grows in a wild state, but
some attempt at cultivation has been made in Malaya. To gather
it the natives sever the branches with a small axe, their hands
being encased with thick hide gloves to protect them from the
thorns. The branches are then allowed to remain where they hang
so that the sun will loosen and shrivel up the sheath or outer
bark, which facilitates its removal. This is done in an ingenious
manner: a notch is cut in the side of a trunk of a neighbouring
tree, and through this the cane is drawn, which removes the
outer bark. The inner bark consists of a very hard, glossy surface
or rind; this is not separate, but part of the cane. After the canes
are cut into lengths of from 12 ft. to 30 ft. they are tied up in
bundles and taken down the river to the 'godown', or native
warehouse, and then shipped to Singapore, where they are graded
into their various sizes and qualities, and sold to agents who dis-
patch them mainly to China, America, Germany, Holland, and
also to France and England. Pulp cane is made from the first
qualities of cane called 'segas', a fine glossy surfaced cane also
known to the trade as 'Sarawak'. This produces the best pulp
cane on account of its pliability and good colour. The term 'pulp'
is misleading, as it is the centre or core of the rattan, which is
very tough and fibrous and not at all pulpy.

The manufacture of pulp cane, or centre cane as it is often
called, grew in quite an interesting way.

Glossy or chair-seating cane—the outside or rattan—originally came from China, and was used for the backs and seats of chairs from the seventeenth century. During the eighteenth century very fine work of this kind was done in France, and beautiful and wonderfully constructed bamboo chairs with fine cane seats came from China. When this chair-seating cane was first made in Europe the centres were mostly treated as waste, except where they were used for cricket bat handles and whips.

This waste was ultimately split into thin round (pulp) cane and found suitable for chair-making, etc., the furniture thus made being painted or varnished. Most of the designs made were foolish and ugly until about 1890, when some German and Austrian architects turned their attention to this medium for furniture design and produced a variety of straightforward but rather angular types of chairs, tables, settees, lamps, work baskets, etc. This work was introduced occasionally into England, but did not assort with English ideas of comfort or design.

The first successful attempts at an English style of pulp cane furniture grew out of some experiments carried out in 1906 at the Leicester Art School by the late Mr. B. J. Fletcher and Mr. Charles Crampton, the writer of this book, who belongs to an old basket-making family. These experiments led to the starting of the Dryad Works in 1907 and the making of a straightforward and simply designed but comfortable cane furniture, which has since become so popular and caused a revival of this industry in England and America.

The process of making pulp cane is as follows. First the selected canes are washed so as to bring out to its best advantage the beauty of the silicated surface. Then the leaf ridges, or 'shots', as they are called, are smoothed down and the cane is passed through a machine with rollers, which press the cane against knives. The knives split and strip the outer surface of the cane into fine narrow strips, which are planed on the back and sides, and this is used for the weaving of bedroom chair seats, etc. The cane core is again put through another machine and split into various sizes. These will vary according to the size of the holes in the knives and thickness required, and will range from less than 1 mm. to 18 mm. in diameter. Other machines cut or split the cane into various shapes, such as square, half-round, flat or bevelled. The highest grade of cane splitting is done in Germany and America, but it is also split in France, Holland, Italy, and to a small extent in England. The Chinese pulp cane is mostly made by hand and is very rough and poor in quality—the outer rough, glossy strands are used there for covering ginger jars, and coarser kinds for cotton baling. The Chinese still make chair-seating cane by hand, but the quality is usually poor. The solid roots of the cane, which resemble those of bamboo, are made into polo balls and mallets, as they are lighter than wood, and owing to the knotted grain will not split easily.

Apart from coal, wool and cotton skeps, hampers, chairs, baskets, etc., cane has been used for whips, bat handles, tennis racket handles, hat brims, beer barrel spigots, trunk-making, upholstery beading on motor-cars, etc.

The waste fibre from cane splitting is twisted into mats by prison labour on the Continent, or used for cheap upholstery stuffing.

The natives use cane for suspension bridges, huts and stockades, fishing traps and elephant gear, tying teak rafts together, sleeping mats, etc.

There are very many varieties of the cane palm. Sixty are recorded by the Government Forestry Department, Kuala Lumpur, Malaya, and about three hundred species are known.

Cane is also found in West Africa and other tropical countries, and is used by the natives for rough basket-work. A missionary on the Congo had some photographs of well-designed chairs made by trained native labour from materials growing in the neighbourhood. African cane generally is of low quality, rough outer surface, no gloss, coarse grain, and all liable to kink.

As the trade names often cover several kinds of cane, it is difficult to connect them with the native and botanical names. However, a few trade names and general description and uses are given.

TOHITI. A thick cane from 12 mm. to 30 mm. in diameter, used for frames of furniture and stiffening hampers.

SARAWAK. A fine, yellow glossy-surfaced cane 8 mm. to 18 mm. This is used for furniture and basket-making. The outer part is used for making chair seating, the inner for pulp cane, bat handles, etc.

PALEMBANG, named after a port in Java. This covers a variety of small canes 3 mm. to 8 mm. in diameter, usually of a red brown colour, slightly ribbed surface. The coarser varieties are used for hampers and baskets; the finer, after being washed, are used for chairs.

BOONDOOT. Similar cane, but harder and lighter in colour.

SEGAH (*Calamus Caesius*). A cane 4 mm. to 10 mm., fine glossy surface, used for pulp cane and glossy chair seating.

KOOBOO (Malay for a trap or stockade usually made of cane). A yellow, glossy, soft-natured cane used for hampers, 5 mm. to 12 mm.

MALACCA CANE (*Rotan Semambu*) (*Calamus Scipionum*) is another variety which is not quite round and has a slight rib on one side. This cane is used largely for walking sticks, because of the wide space between the leaf joints, and it is stiffer than rattan. Extreme examples have joints sixty inches apart. These canes are also used for drain rods and sweeps' canes. The notches, or leaf joints, are much larger than on rattans.

NILGHIRI. A very hard cane, difficult to bend, and used mainly for walking sticks. This cane grows in India. Other walking stick canes are Whangee, Dragon Canes, Partridge Canes, etc.

BIBLIOGRAPHY

CANE AND WILLOW BASKETRY, AND HISTORY

The Junior Basket Maker, by Charles Crampton. (Dryad Press.)
Willow Basketwork, by A. G. Knock. (Dryad Press.)
'Basket-Making', by Thomas Okey. (*R.S.A. Journal*, 11.1.1907.)
The Art of Basket-making, by Thomas Okey. (Pitman.)
Records of the Basketmakers' Company, compiled by H. H. Bobart, M.B.E. (Dunn Collin & Co., St. Mary Axe, E.C.)
Basketwork Through the Ages, by H. H. Bobart, M.B.E. (Oxford University Press, 1936.)
Lehrbuch für Korbflechter, by Gustav Funke. (Franz Deuticke, Vienna.) Has an interesting list of materials.
Manuel de Vannerie, by Eug. Leroux and R. Duchesne. (Librairie J. B. Baillière et Fils, Paris.)
Chinese Baskets, by Berthold Laufer, Curator of Anthropology. (Field Museum of Natural History, Chicago.)
Some Technological Notes from the Pomeroon District, British Guiana, by Dr. Walter E. Roth. Part III. (Royal Anthropological Institute of Great Britain and Ireland, London.)
'Some Commercial Notes on Baskets', by Hugo H. Miller. (Page 485 of *The Philippine Craftsman*, January 1914. Published by Bureau of Education, Manila.)

CANE AND ITS GROWTH

British Empire Exhibition, Rattan Malayan Records, XVII.
Common Products of India, by Sir G. Watt. (Murray, 1908.)
A Manual of Indian Timbers, by J. S. Gamble. 2nd edition. (Sampson Low, 1922.) Gives list of canes, p. 734.
Kew Bulletin, 1899, p. 200.
Malayan Forest Records, No. 2, 1922.
De Nuttige Planten van Nederlandsch-Indie, by K. Heyne. Part I, Batavia, 1911.
Agricultural Bulletin of the Straits and Federated Malay States, No. 2, by H. N. Ridley. (Singapore, 1903.) Pp. 129-136, 159-160.

WILLOW AND ITS GROWTH

A Monograph of the British Willows, by Rev. E. F. Linton, M.A. (West, Newman & Co., 1913.)
Cultivation of Osiers and Willows, by W. P. Ellmore (Dent, 1919.)
Cultivation of Osiers and Willows, Board of Agriculture and Fisheries Miscellaneous Publications, No. 18. (H.M. Stationery Office, 1913.)
Korbweidenbau, by von Wissmann. (Deutsche Landwirtschafts-Gesells., Berlin, 1928.)
Korbweidenbau und Bandstockbetriebe, by E. Kern. (Oberleutnant Kern, Osnabruck, 1904.)
Osiériculture, by E. Leroux. (Librairie J.-B. Baillière, Paris, 1921.)
Rural Industries of England and Wales. Vols. I and IV. (Oxford Press.)

INDIAN BASKETRY AND HISTORY

Indian Basketry, by Otis Tufton Mason, Curator, Division of Ethnology, U.S. National Museum. (William Heinemann, London.) 2 vols. Copiously illustrated in colour and line.
Indian Basketry and How to Make Baskets, by George Wharton James. Henry Malkan, New York.)
Poetry and Symbolism of Indian Basketry, by George Wharton James. (George Wharton James, Pasadena, Cal.)
'*The Ancient Basket Makers of South-eastern Utah*', by George H. Pepper. (Supplement to *American Museum Journal*, April 1902.)
Basketry of the Papago and Pima, by Mary Lois Kissell. Anthropological Papers of the American Museum of Natural History, Vol. XVII, Part IV. (Published by order of the Trustees, New York.)
Iroquois Foods and Food Preparation, by F. W. Waugh. No. 12, Anthropological Series, Department of Mines, Canada. (Government Printing Bureau, Ottawa.)
The Pima and His Basket, by J. F. Breazeale. (Arizona Archæological and Historical Society, Tucson.)
Pine-Needle Basketry in Schools, by William C. A. Hammel. Department of the Interior Bureau of Education Bulletin No. 3, 1917. (Government Printing Office, Washington.)

CHAPTER III

HINTS FOR THE WORKER: MATERIALS, TOOLS AND TECHNICAL TERMS

It is important that the following hints should be carefully studied before proceeding to the practical work, so that they can be applied as required in the working of the various examples. One of the main points to remember in basket-making is that the cane should never be worked dry, for in doing so its capabilities and qualities are sacrificed. It is not necessary to soak the cane, but sufficient to pass it through water and allow it to lie a few minutes before using, damping it again as it becomes dry during the working.

The worker should determine the easiest and most comfortable position for working, and the two following are recommended:

(*a*) The most usual one adopted, particularly by men workers, is sitting with a light board resting on the floor and against the knees. This will be in a sloping position and is much more satisfactory than working on a flat board. The bottom of the basket is pegged to the board with a bradawl, letting the edge of the base be level with the upper edge of the board. The work can be much more easily handled in this position, as the basket will revolve easily during the process of weaving. Also, the work can easily be seen and any irregularity corrected at once (see Fig. 14, page 30).

(*b*) Women and girl workers usually prefer to use a sloping work board placed on a table, as illustrated in the lower half of Fig. 14. This consists of two pieces of wood 12 in. long by 8 in. wide, and 6 in. long by 8 in. wide, nailed together in the position shown. The raised end must face the worker, and the basket is pegged on the board with the edge of the base and this coinciding. All weaving is worked from left to right. The size and shape of a basket should be decided at the start, and it is important that these should be strictly adhered to, as unless care is taken it is quite easy, and most probable, for the worker to depart entirely from them.

Trays can be worked on a flat surface and do not require pegging.

Fig. 14. CORRECT POSITION FOR WORKING

The beginner is advised to start with a wooden base, as he is thus enabled to master the various strokes and the correct way of using his fingers. The wood will also give the article a firm foundation. Only after a little experience should a basket with a cane base be attempted, as the foundation must be firm, as in all constructional work. When a cane base is made it should be slightly curved, like an inverted saucer, as this gives firmness and strength, and has more power of resistance than a perfectly flat one. To give extra strength to the bottom of a basket, when commencing to weave the sides, the first three rows of upsetting cane can be a little thicker than that used for the randing and thinner than that used for the stakes.

The upsetting must be perfectly level before starting the ordinary weaving or randing, and for this purpose a rapping iron is used (see Description of Tools, page 36).

In making a cane base care should be taken to arrange the stakes at equal distances apart at the beginning, as this will help to ensure regularity in the spacing of the upright stakes of the basket, which is essential to good work.

When making a round basket with a cane base, after the stakes have been bent up and shaped for the sides it is helpful for a beginner to place a ring of cane over the stakes so that they rest inside it, thus preventing the natural tendency for them to spread outwards. This ring can be removed when the stakes have been set in position by the weaving. A 10 in. ring is a convenient size, made from a length of No. 12 cane twisted together in a threefold manner.

Where a wooden base is used there is always a tendency at the beginning of the upsetting to draw the work in. It is therefore advisable to press the stakes outwards slightly to prevent this. Also, when damping the cane, care must be taken not to wet the wood, and if this does happen, it should be wiped at once, as even clean water will leave a stain. The underside should be rubbed with a damp cloth, which will prevent the wood from warping, as this is caused by one side only getting damp, and thus if both sides are wetted there is an equal pull on the wood.

When the side of a basket is to slope outwards, the stakes should be arranged fairly close together at the base, otherwise they will be found to be too far apart at the top edge when ready for bordering.

The ends of the cane should not be cut off until the work is finished, and care should be taken not to cut them too short, or the work will be spoilt, nor should they be left too long. In cutting cane a very sharp knife is far less liable to slip and do damage than a duller one. It is sometimes safer to use a small pair of clippers or hand shears.

When the work is completed it should be singed with a Bunsen gas burner or a methylated spirit lamp to remove all the thin fibres. A wax taper should not be used, as this blackens the cane.

All basket work is greatly inproved if washed with warm water. Never use soap.

All cane should be allowed to dry before being stored away, as otherwise it will become discoloured.

Beginners often make the work too strenuous by gripping the canes too tightly, thus making the fingers very sore. This can be avoided if during the working the canes are carefully placed in position and held there lightly, in most cases with the left hand, while the stroke is being made with the right.

In all methods of weaving the fingers of the left hand should be placed between the stakes, one in each space, with the thumb resting on the weaving cane immediately against the stake round which the cane is to pass. The middle finger of the right hand is placed between this stake and the next one, to draw the cane through in the form of a loop so that the stake remains upright during the process and is not bent forward out of position.

The worker is advised not to use too long a length of cane, as this becomes ravelled and dirty. A length should not exceed three yards. The joining of the lengths is quite a simple matter, and is explained later.

The lengths of cane in the bundles supplied are from 14 ft. to 20 ft. These are bent in half for convenience, and as it is almost impossible to straighten the bend it is best to cut this portion from the entire bundle for a depth of 1 in., thus making the canes of a practical length for use.

To store the cane either lay it flat in a rack or bend the lengths into half, making a broad loop, and after tying the ends loosely together hang it up in some convenient place. Never store it

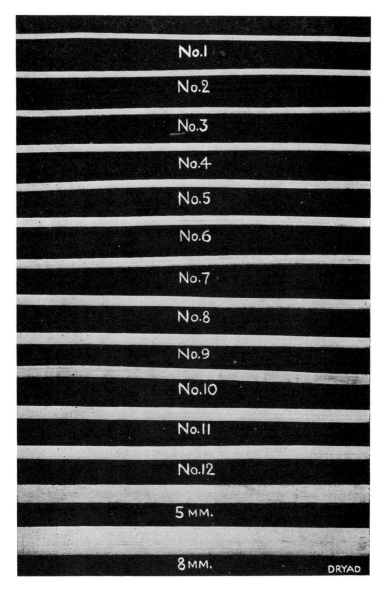

Fig. 15. APPROXIMATE SIZES OF CANE

C

away coiled up or near any hot pipes, as it will become brittle
and crack easily.

Should the cane have been coiled and difficulty be experienced
in straightening it, it should be soaked in water for a few minutes
and hung on a nail to dry, when it will drop out straight.

MATERIALS

As already stated, PULP CANE is the principal material used
for the baskets, etc., described. On page 33 will be found a chart
of the various sizes of pulp cane (actual size). Note that No. 3
cane is approximately 2 mm. thick, and No. 8 cane 3 mm. The
cane can be dyed in various shades, and, used judiciously in
conjunction with natural cane, gives a pleasing effect. Various
materials other than pulp cane can be introduced into the weaving
in basket-making to give variety in colour. These include:

ENAMELLED CANE. A flat cane with a glossy enamelled surface
obtainable in lengths of approximately 2 yds. in a number of
good bright colours.

STRAW PLAIT, which is used for weaving into the cheaper type
of baskets over cane stakes. As it is about ½ in. wide the weaving
is quickly done.

TWISTED SEAGRASS. Of natural bronze green colour, used for
weaving over cane stakes. Can be also obtained dyed in bright
colours.

RUSH. Of a bronze green colour in lengths varying from 4 ft. to
6 ft., tapering at one end. This is effective either used in its
natural state or in the form of a plait.

WOODEN BASES

Trays and various baskets are most practical made with wooden
bases. These are usually made of oak or birch. Oak is superior in
appearance to the birch because of its pleasant, natural grain.
Birch is a plain white wood, slightly lower in cost than the oak,
and is very useful for inexpensive bases for school work and
beginners. Bases can, however, be made of any non-warpable
plywood, or any of the strong new plastic materials.

Coloured bases sometimes look attractive, particularly for
trays. These can be stained and polished, or painted with enamel
(both of which can be sponged), as follows:

STAINING. The base must have a perfectly smooth surface before the stain is applied. This is done by rubbing the surface with sandpaper, first using a medium size and then a very fine one.

All dust must be removed from the base before staining.

Stains are usually supplied in powder form and mixed with boiling water according to the directions on the tin. The stain is applied with a fairly soft brush, and in applying it the brush should follow the grain of the wood.

When thoroughly dry the surface must be rubbed down again with the fine sandpaper, ready for applying the polish.

The temperature and atmosphere of the room in which french polishing is done are very important as good work cannot be done in a cold or damp room. The temperature should be about 70°.

Give the base a coating of the french polish with a brush. This will soak into the wood and act as a filler. Leave it for about an hour to dry thoroughly and then lightly sandpaper again with the fine sandpaper. See that the base is quite free from dust and then commence to apply the polish with a pad made of wadding covered with muslin. The muslin should not contain any dressing and should therefore be washed before using.

Soak the pad with polish but do not have it too wet. Dip the fingers into linseed oil and dab a little on the bottom of the pad. Then commence to rub in a series of small circular movements over the surface of the base, working first from left to right and then back again from right to left, just overlapping the first portion and continuing to and fro in this manner until the entire surface is covered. As the pad dries more polish must be applied and a little more linseed oil as the polish begins to pull, but only a minimum amount of the latter.

When several applications have been made the base must be allowed to stand for at least two or three hours to let the polish sink into the wood.

The last operation in french polishing, which gives the final gloss, is known as 'spiriting off'. This removes all marks and smears. Instead of adding more polish to the pad, add a little methylated spirit (no linseed oil). The pad is then applied very lightly so as not to pull up the previous coats of polish, and more methylated spirit must be added as required. The direction of the pad should now be straight with the grain of the wood and not circular as before.

If preferred, the staining can be omitted and the bases just polished as described, which slightly darkens the colour of the wood.

ENAMELLING. Birch has a finer grain than oak and is therefore preferable for enamelling.

The surface must be quite smooth as before and rubbed over with sandpaper.

A special quick-drying enamel is recommended, which is applied with a fairly soft brush in the usual manner. Two or three coats are necessary, each fresh coat to be applied when the previous one is thoroughly dry, which takes about half an hour.

The enamel should be well stirred before using and again once or twice during its application so that its full strength is obtained.

Where any quantity of bases are to be stained or enamelled, a small handspray can be bought fairly inexpensively for applying the stain and enamel. Besides being a more speedy method, it ensures a perfectly smooth surface free from brush marks and other blemishes.

TOOLS

As regards tools, an expensive outfit is not necessary, but most of the following are essential for good work with minimum difficulty:

ROUND-NOSED PLIERS for squeezing or bruising the stakes so that they can be bent for bordering at an acute angle without cracking.

SHEARS for cutting a number of stakes together and for cutting off the ends inside a basket. In some places this is preferable to using a knife.

SMALL BODKIN to make the necessary space for inserting stakes into a cane base or for threading the ends of border canes, etc.

SHARP KNIFE. Essential for cutting off ends and for pointing stakes, etc.

PICKING KNIFE for cutting off all randing ends when article is finished.

BENT BODKIN. A very useful tool for making the necessary space in a basket for inserting a handle.

BRADAWL for pegging a cane base to a board so that it can be turned round freely.

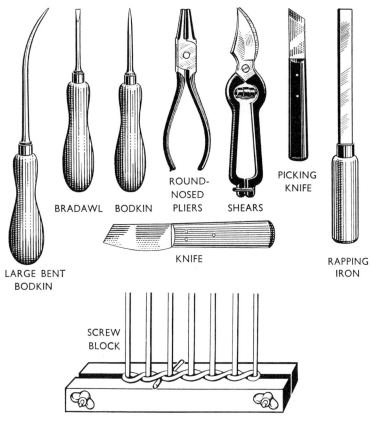

Fig. 16

RAPPING IRON to tap the rows of weaving to make the work quite level.

SCREWBLOCK for holding the stakes rigid in making a rectangular base.

AN EXPLANATION OF THE TECHNICAL TERMS USED IN BASKET-MAKING

STAKES. The upright or foundation canes on which the weaving is done.

BYE-STAKES. Additional stakes inserted by the side of the original stakes to give extra strength. These are used in most cases in preference to single thicker stakes, as they give a flatter and less clumsy appearance to the finished article.

UPSETTING. The three or four rows of weaving worked at the commencement of the side of a basket to 'set' the stakes in order, i.e. at equal distance apart and at the required angle. Where a cane base is used the first row must always be worked with four canes to cover the bending up of the stakes for the sides. The other two or three rows are worked with three canes.

RANDING. Weaving with a single cane.

PAIRING. Weaving with two canes which are worked alternately, using the left-hand one each time, placing it before and behind one stake alternately.

WALING. Upsetting with three canes is called waling, when used in any other part of a basket.

SLEWING. Worked in the same way as the randing, but two or more canes are used for each row instead of one.

BORDERS :

TRAC BORDERS. Borders in which each stake is bent down in turn, entirely completing its necessary movements or strokes before bending down the next stake, which is contrary to most borders where one stake helps to complete the movement of the others.

THREE-ROD PLAIN BORDER. The most common type of closed border, used on trays and baskets.

BACK TRAC. An additional border worked with the remaining ends of a three-rod plain border in the opposite direction to the border.

FOLLOW-ON-TRAC. Also worked with the remaining ends of a three-rod plain border, but in the same direction as the border.

FOOT BORDER. Worked under wooden bases of trays and baskets.

SCALLOPED BORDER. An open type of border used on small baskets where strength is not essential.

PLAITED BORDER. A closed border in which the canes are worked in the form of a plait; used for trays, baskets, etc.

CHAPTER IV

METHODS OF WEAVING

To save repetition, the various methods of weaving and the working of the different types of borders and handles will be described collectively in the next three chapters. They can be referred to then as they occur later in the instructions given for the finished examples of canework.

Fig. 17. THREE-ROD UPSETTING OR THREE-ROD WALE. Place three canes between the stakes in three consecutive spaces with the ends pointing inside to the left, protruding about 1 in. Take the left-hand cane of the three and pass it in front of two stakes, over the other two canes, and behind one, bringing it to the front again as in diagram.

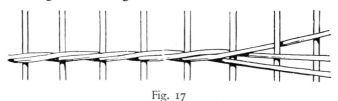

Fig. 17

Continue in this way, taking the left-hand cane each time, until the starting-point of the row is reached; that is, when the last used cane comes out, on the left of the first stake.

This cane is worked in front of two stakes and behind one, then the next cane is worked in a similar manner, and the last one also.

Now the three canes are ready to proceed with the next row in the usual way. This is completed in the same way as the first, and also any further rows so that each one appears complete in itself.

When the desired number of rows are worked, instead of making the step-up for a further row take the left-hand cane one more stroke forward in the usual way. This cane is now finished off. Then take the left-hand cane of the two remaining, over two stakes and behind one stake and under one weaving cane and out to the front, and the third cane over two stakes and behind one stake and under *two* weaving canes and out to the front. Trim off the ends.

In pairing and waling, the finish of ends simply means that the pattern must be carried out and the ends must finish where they began, no matter what type of wale is being worked.

Fig. 18. FOUR-ROD UPSETTING. Squeeze two lengths of cane at the centre, and bend them into half to make four canes. Place these, at the bend, round two alternate stakes. Take the extreme left-hand cane and pass it in front of three stakes, and behind one, bringing it to the front again, and repeat in this way until the starting-point of the row is reached, that is, when the last used cane comes out in the same place as the first cane; cut it off, so that only 1 in. remains, as it will not be required again.

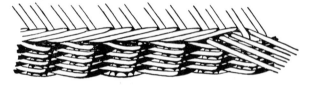

Fig. 18

Complete the pattern of the row by taking the right-hand cane in front of the three stakes, and behind one, and the other two canes in turn in the same manner. When this has been done the three canes are ready to proceed with the three-rod upsetting in the usual way, as described above. This, however, should be worked on the knee for two or three rows, to enable the stakes to be placed at an angle of 45 degrees.

Fig. 19. RANDING. Place the end of a length of cane between two stakes with the end pointing inside to the left. Pass this in front of one stake, and behind one, until the row is complete. If there is an odd number of stakes, the weaving can be continued with the same cane in the next row, and onwards to the required depth, so that where the cane passes in front of the stakes in the first row, it will pass behind these in the next row, and so on. If however, there is an even number of stakes, the weaving is only made correct by inserting another length of cane for the second row, in the space to the left of the starting-point of the first row.

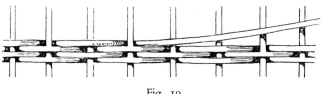

Fig. 19

The two canes are then used for the alternate rows, i.e. the first cane will be used for the third row and the second for the fourth, and so on. They must not, however, be allowed to overtake each other, which means that as soon as the cane of the previous row is reached, the cane in use must be left and the work continued with the other cane.

Fig. 20. PAIRING. Squeeze a length of cane at the centre and bend it in half to make two canes. Place it round a stake at the bend with the canes pointing outside to the right. Take the left-hand cane, pass it over the right-hand cane and behind the next stake, so that actually it will have passed in front of one stake (the first stake) and behind one. Repeat in this way, using the left-hand cane each time, passing in front of one stake, over the right-hand cane, and behind one. The finishing of the final row must be immediately over the starting-point, and the ends of the two canes must be threaded into the beginning of the row so that the working is continuous and the join unnoticeable.

Fig. 20

Fig. 21. CHAIN PAIRING. The chain effect is obtained by working the alternate rows of pairing in a different manner as follows: Work round the basket with ordinary pairing first and draw the ends of cane through by the side of the starting-point, to complete the row. Cut them off so that only $\frac{1}{2}$ in. remains Start again at any point with two more canes, but this time from the inside of the basket. Insert two weaving canes between the stakes in two consecutive spaces, with ends protruding about an inch on the outside of the basket and pointing to the left. Work from the outside of the basket and take the left-hand cane from inside the basket, behind one stake to the outside of the basket and over one stake and through to the inside again, and leave it there. Repeat the stroke with both canes until you have the whole row worked. Then complete by drawing both ends through to the inside where the first two ends start the pairing. Repeat these two rows alternately as often as required.

Fig. 21

A very effective pattern can be obtained by using two pairs of canes, instead of two single ones, letting each pair consist of one coloured and one plain one. These must be placed side by side so that both canes touch the stakes.

In the first row let the coloured cane be below the plain one, but in the second row let the coloured cane be the top one so that the two plain canes are in the centre of the 'chain'. The two pairs of canes are used in turn in this way, one pair for a row of ordinary pairing and one pair for a row of reverse pairing.

Fig. 22. CHAIN WALING. Here, again, each alternate row is worked in a reverse manner to obtain the chain effect. Work round the basket with ordinary waling and draw the ends through by the side of the starting-point to complete the row. Cut the canes off so that they are only $\frac{1}{2}$ in. long.

Start again at any point with three more canes as before, but this time from the inside of the basket. Place three canes between

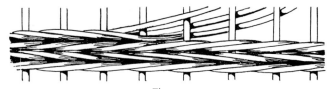

Fig. 22

the stakes in three consecutive spaces with ends protruding about an inch on the outside of the basket and pointing to the left. Working from the outside of the basket, take the left-hand cane from the inside of basket, behind one stake, passing to the outside, then over two stakes and through to the inside of the basket. Repeat this stroke with all three canes until the row has been worked, and complete by drawing the finishing ends through where three ends start the wale. Repeat rows as required. Chain waling, like the chain pairing, can also be worked with pairs of coloured and plain canes, and makes a bold pattern suitable for introducing into the sides of a waste-paper basket.

Fig. 23. FITCHING. The name given to the row of working added to the top edge of a band of openwork to hold the canes forming this in the required position. Fig. 23 shows a border in which the bye-stakes are bent over to form small crosses, each right-hand bye-stake being brought to the next stake on the right, and each left bye-stake to the next stake on the left so that each stake will again have two bye-stakes. The three canes in each case require to be held closely together, and a row of fitching is therefore worked for the purpose as follows. Squeeze

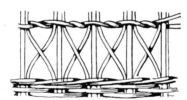

Fig. 23

a length of soft cane at the centre and bend it in half to make two canes. Place this round one of the stakes with its two bye-stakes, twist the back cane over the front one and then pass it behind the next stake and bye-stakes, letting the front cane pass in front of these. Then twist the back cane over the front one again, and so on. By making this twist, each stake with its two bye-stakes will be firmly and separately held in position.

To finish off the ends of a single fitch, simply carry on the end into the randing or waling above it. However, in the case of a double fitch, as shown in Fig. 24, the centre fitch should have two rows of canes and the ends should be threaded away to the inside of the basket.

Fig. 24. FITCHING. Here there is no crossing or changing of the position of the bye-stakes, and so the row of fitching can be worked like a row of pairing, without the extra twist, which is not required to adjust or separate the bye-stakes into a new position as in the previous openwork pattern.

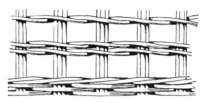

Fig. 24

Fig. 25. SLEWING. As previously described, this is merely randing with two or more canes. Coloured cane can be introduced if desired, in which case either one coloured cane with a plain one on either side of it can be used, or two coloured canes and one plain one. Care must be taken to keep an even tension on all the canes in use so that the work appears regular.

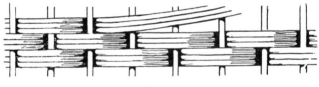

Fig. 25

To start slewing, take one stroke with one cane, then add another and similarly a third cane to make the start gradual. Finish off in the same manner.

METHODS OF ADDING A NEW LENGTH OF CANE

RANDING. Leave the remaining end of the used length of cane inside, pointing to the right, place the new end over this in a crosswise position pointing inside to the left, Fig. 26. As the work

Fig. 26

proceeds these ends will be made quite secure and can be cut off quite close to the work.

UPSETTING, WALING AND PAIRING. Leave the remaining end of the used length of cane pointing outwards, and insert the end of the new cane in the same space by the side of it, pointing inwards.

Fig. 27. SAMPLER BASKET OF WEAVES. The photograph on page 46 shows a sampler basket made up of different weaves, introducing various materials. Details of these are given below this. It is very helpful to make a basket of this description to use as a reference for future work, and particularly convenient for the teacher to have this collection of specimens in such a compact form to show to students. It should, of course, be mentioned that it is not intended to be an example of a finished basket, being much too elaborate and fussy; incidentally it serves to show the mistake of using too many different weaves in one piece of work.

Fig. 27. SAMPLER BASKET OF WEAVES (See pages 39-45)

1 Three-rod upsetting (4 rows)
2 Randing
3 Three-rod waling (2 rows)
4 Alternate rows of flat and round cane
5 Chain waling
6 Alternate rows straw plait and round cane
7 Chain waling
8 Pairing with dyed and natural pulp cane
9 Three-rod waling (2 rows)

10 Double cane chain pairing
11 Three-rod waling (2 rows)
12 Seagrass and slewing
13 Three-rod waling (2 rows)
14 Double cane chain waling
15 Three-rod waling (2 rows)
16 Slewing with a dyed and natural cane
17 Three-rod waling
18 Plaited border (two-rod five-stroke)

4, 6, 8 and 12 require an even number of stakes.

CHAPTER V

BORDERS

Many amateurs who enjoy making baskets find that their real difficulty lies in working the border. Appreciating the difficulty of learning to do basket-work from written instructions, the working of the following borders is described in the hope that it will make the bordering of a basket more simple. The stakes must all be thoroughly damp and pliable before starting to work. The scallop or open border is the simplest to work, but it is wise not to adopt this for baskets which are intended for hard wear. The closed border is much stronger and more durable as it adds firmness to the sides of a basket, and with this there is less likelihood of ends becoming loose.

POINTS TO REMEMBER. To make a firm border the stakes must not be arranged too far apart.

Two or three rows of waling should be worked with cane a size less than the stakes, before bordering, to strengthen the shape of the basket, so that it will not easily be altered during the working of the border.

In describing the borders it is assumed that No. 6 cane is used for the stakes of the baskets. Where a thinner or thicker cane has been used the depth allowed in squeezing the stakes for a trac border must be altered accordingly.

Care should be taken to gauge the beginning correctly and to see that the finishing strokes are woven into the beginning, carefully following the pattern of the border, so that the joining point is in no way visible.

All borders are worked from left to right.

Finally, the borders are not as difficult as they at first appear, for in all cases they are merely the repetition of one or two simple strokes.

Fig. 28. SIMPLE SCALLOP OR OPEN BORDER. Suitable for small baskets, dinner mats, glass-holders, etc. Hard cane is better for the stakes than soft when making this type of border, as it will bend more evenly and be less inclined to kink.

Each stake is bent over and inserted by the side of the next

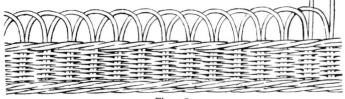

Fig. 28

but one stake, passing it in front of the intermediate stake each time (see illustration).

The loops should be $\frac{7}{8}$ in. deep and of uniform shape. To ensure this, make one loop, first inserting the cane well down the basket, and then measure the length required. Cut off all the stakes to this measurement, point the ends for inserting and proceed with the border.

Fig. 29. SCALLOP BORDER. This is worked in a similar way to Fig. 28, but here each stake passes in front of two stakes and is inserted through the wale midway between the third and fourth stakes.

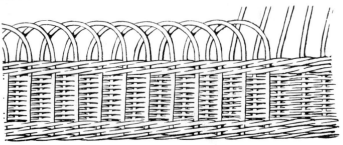

Fig. 29

An interesting effect can be obtained with this border by allowing the ends of the cane, after they have been brought through the wale, to pass in front of the randing and then be inserted again at the base through the rows of upsetting as shown.

Fig. 30. TRAC BORDER, SINGLE STAKE. This is the simplest of the closed borders and is suitable for small baskets. The stakes should measure about 4 in. above the waling. Squeeze the first stake with round-nosed pliers about $\frac{1}{2}$ in. above the tip of the wale to allow space for the final strokes of the border. Bend this down behind one stake, before one, behind one, and before one, leaving the ends inside. Repeat, squeezing and working each stake in turn in the same way, carefully threading the finishing strokes of the border so that the pattern is continuous. Cut off all projecting ends.

Fig. 30

Fig. 31. TRAC BORDERS, DOUBLE STAKES. Suitable for small work baskets, hand baskets, etc.

It is not necessary here to squeeze the stakes with the pliers. Take the first double stake and bend it down rather sharply at a height of about $\frac{5}{8}$ in. above the wale, and pass it behind one stake and in front of two, leaving the ends inside. Work the other stakes in the same way, taking care to keep the border the same depth throughout. Finish off the ends correctly by threading into the first stakes.

The stakes should measure about 4 in. above the wale where the stakes are approximately $\frac{3}{4}$ in. apart.

Fig. 31

Fig. 32. TRAC BORDER WITH DOUBLE STAKES. Suitable for work baskets, shopping baskets, etc. This is worked in a similar way to border, Fig. 30, but here the stakes are double, and in the illustration the first stake is taken in front of the next, and so on, instead of behind, as described for Fig. 30. This is not essential, however, but can be worked either way. The stakes are bent down about $1\frac{1}{8}$ in. above the wale. If, after working a few strokes, it is found that the stakes should have been bent at a greater or less distance, undo the working and start again correctly.

D

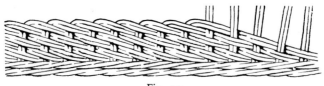

Fig. 32

Fig. 33. TRAC BORDER WITH DOUBLE STAKES. Suitable for larger baskets, as it has a heavier appearance than the previous borders. The stakes should measure about 6 in. above the wale where the stakes are approximately $\frac{5}{8}$ in. apart, and longer if wider apart. Each double stake is bent down about $1\frac{1}{8}$ in. above the wale, and then passed behind one stake, before two, behind one and before two, leaving the ends inside. The ends must be finished off correctly, threading in and out of the first few stakes to complete the border.

Fig. 33

Fig. 34. THREE-ROD PLAIN BORDER. Suitable for small baskets and oak trays, and is the simplest of the plain borders.

Squeeze all the stakes with the pliers level with the work. Bend down the first stake behind the second, the second stake behind the third, and the third stake behind the fourth. Now pass the first cane bent down over the other two canes, in front of the fourth stake and behind the fifth. Bend down the fourth stake by the right-hand side of this so that both canes are resting flat on the work, and not one on top of the other. Now take the second and third stakes which were bent down and treat them in turn in the same way. There will now be three pairs of

Fig. 34

canes on the front. Take the fifth of these canes, counting from the right, and pass it in front of the next upright stake behind the next and through to the front again. Bend down the appropriate cane alongside it. Continue in this way until there is only one stake left upright (Fig. 34A), then take the fifth cane again in front of this stake and thread it from the inside under the first stake bent down at the starting-point.

Fig. 34A

Now bend the last stake down beside this cane, making a double one as before. The three remaining ends, i.e. the right-hand cane of each pair, are threaded through in their turn to complete the pattern of the border so that there is no join visible.

Finally cut off the protruding ends close to the border.

FOUR-ROD PLAIN BORDER. This is worked in a similar manner to the previous border. Bend down the first, second and third stakes in turn as before, but here bend the fourth stake down also. Then pass the first stake in front of the fifth stake and behind the sixth, after which bend the fifth stake down beside it. Repeat in this way until there are four pairs of canes, then proceed to take the seventh cane, counting from the right, over the other canes and in front of the next upright stake. The border is finished as previously described.

Fig. 35. THREE-ROD PLAIN BORDER WITH BACK TRAC. Suitable for work baskets, paper baskets, oak trays, etc. The stakes should be about $7\frac{1}{2}$ in. above the wale where the stakes are $\frac{5}{8}$ in. apart. The plain border is worked as previously described in Fig. 34, and is completed before the back trac is started. The remaining ends protruding on the outside of the border are not cut off but utilized for the trac border. These are all pointing to the right, and each one must be bent sharply towards the left to make them at right angles to the border. Work on the far side of the basket or tray. Squeeze all stakes for about $\frac{1}{4}$ in. deep to start the trac border and then bend each stake down in turn.

Pass it behind one stake and before two, leaving the ends underneath. When complete the ends are cut off in the usual way.

Fig. 35

PLAITED BORDER, TWO-ROD, THREE-STROKE, Figs. 36-45, suitable for oak trays, work baskets, etc. Squeeze all the stakes with round-nosed pliers and work a two-rod, three-stroke plaited border.

Two short pieces of cane about 3 in. long and three pieces 8 in. long, the same thickness as the stakes, are required.

Place one of the short canes between two stakes pointing to the right. Bend the first stake over it and place an 8 in. piece of cane by the side of this projecting 2½ in. on the inside (see Fig. 36.) Insert another short piece between the next two stakes and bend down No. 2 stake, adding another 8 in. length of cane at the side of it, making two pairs of canes (Fig. 37). Bring the left-hand pair of canes over the next pair and in front of No. 3 stake, leaving the ends inside, so that it actually passes in front of two stakes. Bend No. 3 stake down and place the last of the 8 in. pieces at the side of it. Now pass the left pair of canes again in the same way over these and in front of No. 4 stake, leaving the ends inside, and thus making two pairs of canes on the inside (Fig. 38). Bend No. 4 stake down and then the left inside pair by the side of it, making three canes. Pass the left front pair over these and in front of the next upright stake, which is No. 5, and bend the left inside pair by the side of it. This will make two sets of three canes on the front (Fig. 39), but as only double canes are required the right cane of each group of three canes is omitted throughout the working of the border, and cut off when the border is complete.

Continue the working, first using the left-hand inside pair, and then the left-hand outside pair as described. When the last stake has been bent down and the last pair of canes beside it (Fig. 41), proceed as follows: Remove the first short piece of cane inserted at the beginning, and insert the left-hand front pair of canes in

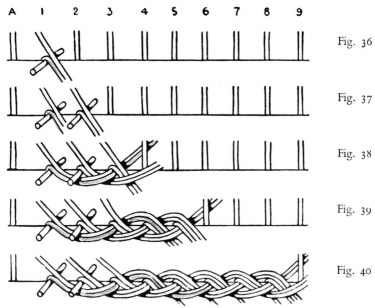

Fig. 36

Fig. 37

Fig. 38

Fig. 39

Fig. 40

its place. Remove the second short piece and insert the remaining pair of canes in the same way. This will make three pairs of canes on the inside pointing to the right and three single canes pointing to the left (Fig. 43). The single canes are threaded by the right-hand side of the three pairs of canes (Fig. 44), and then the inner cane of each pair is threaded by the side of the single canes (Fig. 45). The ends of the cane to be threaded should first be pointed with a knife. The border is now complete and no join will be visible.

Cut off all protruding ends so that the work is quite neat.

Fig. 46. PLAITED BORDER, THREE-ROD, THREE-STROKE. Suitable for trays, work baskets, paper baskets, etc. The stakes should measure $8\frac{1}{2}$ in. above the wale, where the stakes are $\frac{5}{8}$ in. apart. Two short pieces of cane about 3 in. long and six pieces 10 in. long, the same thickness as the stakes, are required. Place one of the short canes between two stakes pointing to the right. Bend the first stake over it and place two 10 in. pieces of cane by the side of this projecting $2\frac{1}{2}$ in. on the inside. Insert another short piece between the next two stakes and bend down No. 2

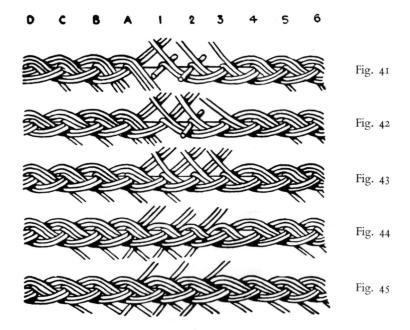

D   C   B   A   1   2   3   4   5   6

Fig. 41

Fig. 42

Fig. 43

Fig. 44

Fig. 45

stake, adding another pair of 10 in. canes at the side of it, making
two groups of three on the front. Bring the left-hand group of
canes over the next group and in front of No. 3 stake, leaving
the ends inside, so that it actually passes in front of two stakes.
Bend No. 3 stake down and place the last pair of 10 in. pieces of
cane at the side of it. Now pass the left-hand group of canes
again in the same way over these and in front of No. 4 stake,
leaving the ends inside, and thus making two groups of three
canes on the inside. Bend No. 4 stake down and then the left
inside group by the side of it, making four canes. Pass the left
front group of three over these and in front of the next upright
stake, which is No. 5, bend down this stake as at No. 3 and No.
4, and bend the left inside three by the side of it. This will make
two sets of four canes on the front, but as only three canes are
required the right-hand cane of each group of four is omitted
throughout the working of the border, and cut off when the
border is complete.

Fig. 46

Continue the working, first using the left-hand group of three canes on the inside of the work, and then the left-hand group of three on the front of the work as described. When the last stake has been bent down and the last group of canes beside it, proceed as follows: Insert the left-hand front three canes into the space where the first short cane was inserted at the beginning of the border, at the same time removing this. Insert the next front three canes into the space containing the second short piece of cane and remove this also. This will make three groups of three canes on the inside pointing to the right and three double canes pointing to the left. The double canes are threaded in turn by the right-hand side of the three groups of three canes, and then the inner cane of each of these groups is threaded by the side of the double ones. The ends of the canes to be threaded should be first pointed with a knife. The border is now complete and no join should be visible. Cut off all protruding ends so that the work is quite neat.

PLAITED BORDER, TWO-ROD, FIVE-STROKE. (See Figs. 47—57 page 56)

The stakes should measure $10\frac{1}{2}$ in. above the wale. Three short pieces of cane about 4 in. long and five pieces $10\frac{1}{2}$ in. long, the same thickness as the stakes, are required. Squeeze all the stakes with the round-nosed pliers.

Place one short piece between two stakes pointing inside to the right. Bend the first stake down over this and place one $10\frac{1}{2}$ in. piece by the side of it, projecting inside about 4 in. (Fig. 47). Insert the other two short pieces in the same way, bending down the second and third stakes in turn and placing a $10\frac{1}{2}$ in. length by the side of each (see Figs. 48 and 49). This will make three pairs of canes on the outside. Place the left thumb under the left-hand side pair of canes and over the other two pairs of canes. Bring the first pair over the other two pairs and in front of the fourth stake, leaving the ends inside, bend down the fourth

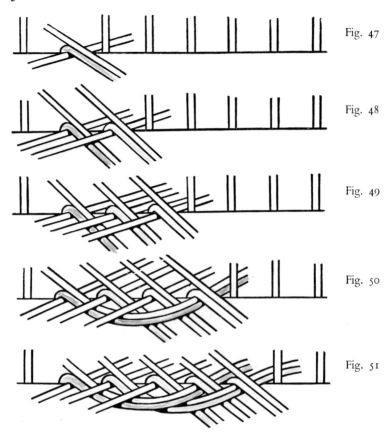

Fig. 47

Fig. 48

Fig. 49

Fig. 50

Fig. 51

stake with the left thumb and place one of the 10½ in. pieces beside it (see Fig. 50).

In a similar way, bring the second pair of canes over and in front of the fifth stake, leaving the ends on the inside as before. Bend down the fifth stake with the left thumb, and add the last 10½ in. cane (see Fig. 51).

There will be two pairs of canes on the inside and three pairs on the outside. Place the left thumb under the first pair (on the left) of the outside canes and over the other two pairs. Pick up the first pair with the right hand and pass it in front of three stakes, leaving the ends inside.

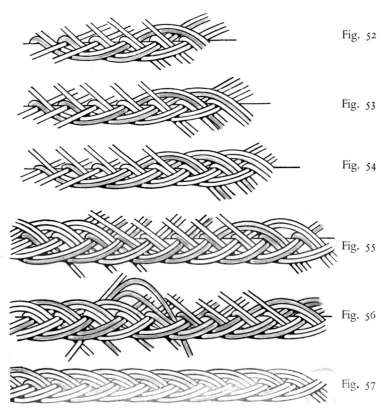

Fig. 52

Fig. 53

Fig. 54

Fig. 55

Fig. 56

Fig. 57

Hold this pair down with the right thumb and place the middle finger of the left hand under the first pair (on the inside) and over the other two pairs, at the same time removing the thumb. Then with the right hand bring the first pair behind two stakes, leaving the ends on the outside. Bend the next stake down beside this pair, making three canes side by side (see Fig. 52). Repeat the whole of this last movement twice, which will make two pairs of canes on the inside and three sets of three canes on the outside (see Figs. 53 and 54).

As only 'pairs' of canes are required, the right-hand cane of each set of three is omitted during the working and cut off when the border is complete. Continue until the last stake has been

bent down beside the last pair of canes. The three short pieces
of cane used at the beginning are now removed in turn as follows:

Remove the first cane and thread the next pair of canes to be
used on the outside into this space, leaving them inside. Now
take the other two pairs in their turn and thread them into the
spaces where the short pieces were. There will now be five pairs
of canes on the inside pointing to the right and five single canes
pointing to the left. The latter must be arranged to come on
top of the former (see Fig. 55). To finish the border thread the
left-hand single cane by the side of the left-hand double cane,
then bring over the right-hand cane of this pair and thread it
by the side of the previous cane (see Fig. 56).

The remaining single and double canes are treated in the same
manner. If neatly worked and threaded, the finish of the border
should not be noticed. All ends must be neatly cut off with a
sharp knife so that when the fingers are rubbed along the underside they cannot be felt.

Fig. 57A. PLAITED BORDER, ONE-ROD FIVE-STROKE.
The stakes should measure about 6 in. above the wale.

Three short pieces of cane, 4 in. long, the same thickness as
the stakes, are required. Squeeze all the stakes with the round-
nosed pliers.

It is advisable to refer to page 57, which gives particulars of
the two-rod five-stroke border, as the one-rod five-stroke border
is carried out in a very similar manner.

Fig. 57A

Place one short piece between two stakes pointing inside to
the right. Bend the first stake down over this. Insert another
short piece over the stake that has been bent down and bend
the second stake down. Treat the third short piece in the same
manner. This will make three single canes on the outside. Place
the left thumb under the left-hand cane and over the other two
canes, Bring the first single cane that was bent down over the
other two and in front of the fourth stake, leaving the end

inside. Bend down the fourth stake with the left thumb, and hold the canes with the right hand. In a similar way, bring the second cane, which is the left-hand one, over and in front of the fifth stake, leaving the end inside as before. Bend down the fifth stake with the left thumb.

There will now be two single canes on the inside and three single canes on the outside. Place the left thumb under the first cane (on the left) of the outside canes and over the other two canes, as previously described. Pick up the first cane with the right hand and pass it in front of three stakes, leaving the ends inside. Hold this cane down with the right thumb and place the middle finger of the left hand under the first cane (on the inside) and over the other two canes, at the same time removing the thumb. Then with the right hand bring the first cane behind two stakes, leaving the end on the outside. Bend the next stake down beside this, making two canes side by side. Repeat the whole of this last movement twice, which will make two single canes on the inside and three sets of two canes on the outside.

As only single canes are required, the right-hand cane of each pair is omitted during the working and cut off when the border is complete. Continue until the last stake has been bent down beside the last cane.

The three short pieces of cane used at the beginning are now removed in turn as follows. Thread the cane that is to be worked next by the side of the first short piece and then remove the short piece, leaving the end inside. Now, take the other two canes in their turn and thread them by the side of the short pieces as just described.

There will now be five single canes on the inside pointing to the right.

To finish the border, thread the left-hand single cane by the side of the first stake that was bent down for the beginning of the border. Repeat these movements for the remaining canes.

If neatly worked and threaded, the finish of the border should not be noticed. All ends must be neatly cut off.

Fig. 58. FOOT BORDER FOR TRAYS AND BASKETS WITH WOODEN BASES. Insert the stakes so that they protrude 4 in. below the base. Turn it with the wrong side uppermost and begin at the centre of one of the long sides. Bend down one stake behind the next and in front of the two following stakes, leaving the ends on the inside to be cut off later. Continue in this way with each stake until the beginning is reached. Before threading the ends of the last stakes through to complete the pattern, ease the first three bent stakes up to make the necessary space for

Fig. 58

them. Make sure they pass behind one stake and in front of two and finish with the ends touching the base.

When the border is complete cut the ends off on the inside quite close to the work.

Fig. 59. THREE-ROD PLAIN BORDER WITH FOLLOW-ON TRAC. The first position is worked the same as border, Fig. 34, but the remaining ends of cane left should be 4 in. long. Make a point at each of these. Pass one end under the next two and insert it between the border and the wale, so that it rests on the back of the stake on the inside. Continue all round in this manner, completing the border by threading the last few ends of cane under the first few canes worked at the beginning.

Fig. 59

Then cut the canes off on the inside so that the ends are just long enough to rest on the stakes. This makes a neat border for trays or shopping baskets.

Fig. 60. WRAPPED BORDER RIM. Some workers may wish to finish their baskets with a wrapped rim similar to the No. 5

work basket illustrated on page 122. For this the method of procedure is as follows:

When the basket has been worked to the required depth, take a length of 8 mm. cane and shape it into a circle to fit the top of the basket. Shave one end gradually to a point on the inside for

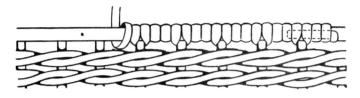

Fig. 60

about 3 in. Place the cane inside the basket, resting on the last row of weaving, and beginning at the pointed end of cane, nail each alternate stake in turn to the cane with $\frac{3}{8}$ in. nails. The final end of the ring must be cut to a point on the outside so that it fits against the first end to make the original thickness of the cane, otherwise it will be bulky when wrapped.

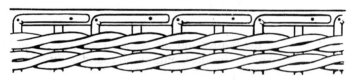

Fig. 61

Cut off the stakes that are not nailed level with the top row of weaving and then squeeze all the remaining stakes with the round-nosed pliers so that they can be bent down level with the circle of cane. Each one is bent in turn to the right and made to rest on the cut end of the other stakes, being cut off close to the next upright stake and nailed to the inside circle (Fig. 61).

If double stakes have been used, cut off the left-hand one of every pair and bend and nail the right-hand one down.

Another length of 8 mm. cane is bent into a circle and nailed on the outside of the stakes, being cut and joined like the first one. Thus a firm regular edge is made ready for wrapping.

During the wrapping the basket is held with the open top

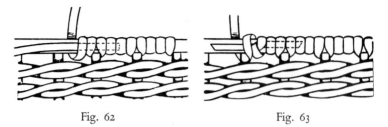

Fig. 62   Fig. 63

facing the worker and the wrapping cane is taken over the edge from left to right away from the worker. Bring the end of the wrapping cane up between the two circles and bend it down along the top. Then proceed to wrap the top edge, at the same time securing the end with the first few wraps.

If the basket has double stakes, one wrap must be made between each pair of stakes, using a bodkin to make way for the cane.

Should it be necessary to join, when about 10 in. only of cane remains, lay a new length of cane along the underside of the frame with the right side nearest to it. Continue wrapping with the old length of cane, taking it over the new cane until only about 2 in. remain (Fig. 62). Now take hold of both the old and the new canes close to the frame and twist them over to the right, thus reversing the position of the canes. Then proceed with the wrapping in the ordinary way, using the new cane (Fig. 63). The joining point should afterwards be tapped with a hammer to make it quite flat.

To secure the final end of wrapping cane thread it under the last loop of the wrapping, pull it tight and put a $\frac{1}{4}$ in. nail through both canes. Then cut off the end of the cane quite close to the wrapping.

If the process of wrapping causes a space between the rim and the last row of waling, a row of waling should be threaded in.

CHAPTER VI

VARIOUS TYPES OF HANDLES FOR BASKETS

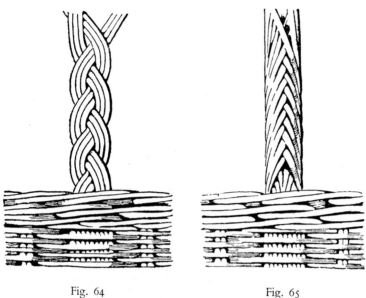

Fig. 64   Fig. 65

Figs. 64 and 65 are only suitable for very small baskets.

Fig. 64. PLAITED, THREE-ROD, THREE-STROKE. Provision must be made during the working of the sides of the basket to take the nine canes which form the handle. This is done by treating the two centre stakes as one stake, randing in front and behind the two to form a pocket where the ends of the handle may be placed. Insert the first of the nine canes in the pocket down to the base of the basket. Bring it out on the front of the work, letting the end protrude for about 3 in. Then insert the other eight canes to the base. Pass the end of the first cane in front of the eight canes and thread it up by the side of the last of the canes. In this way all the canes will be made secure. The nine canes are divided into three groups for plaiting, which is worked in the same way as any ordinary plait. All the canes, however, must be kept side by side so that they are all visible on the surface. When the required length of plait is complete the ends of cane are inserted in the opposite side of the basket in the way already described.

Fig. 65. PLAITED, NINE-ROD, SINGLE-STROKE. Make provision for the handle as in Fig. 64, and insert the nine canes in the same way. Take the outer cane on the left and bend it over the next four canes in a slanting direction, then take the outer one on the right and similarly bend this over four canes, also allowing it to rest on top of the first bent cane. The two outer canes are bent over alternately in this way until the handle is complete, when all the ends are secured in the opposite side of the basket.

Fig. 66. WRAPPED HANDLE, WITH A HERRINGBONE PATTERN. One 8 mm. cane and two 6 mm. canes are required for the handle. These are inserted in the side of the basket, and made secure in either of the two following ways:

(a) A hole is made with a bent bodkin through the side of the handle canes just below the wale of the basket and a small piece of pointed cane is driven into the hole, forming a peg or wedge. The ends of this are then cut off close to the work.

(b) A hole is made through the centre of the cane from the front of the handle and a length of wrapping cane threaded through this, securing the short end along the weaving. The other end is then threaded over the border to form a cross as shown in the illustration. Where the handle is wrapped this cane is used to continue the wrapping, otherwise it is neatly secured in the border.

Care must be taken during this process not to split the handle cane unduly.

When both ends of the handle have been secured the wrapping is started, but before doing so insert a length of No. 10 cane in front of the centre handle cane. The wrapping cane is passed over this together with the handle about four times, after which it is passed under and over alternately as shown in the illustration.

When the wrapping is complete and the ends secured, start

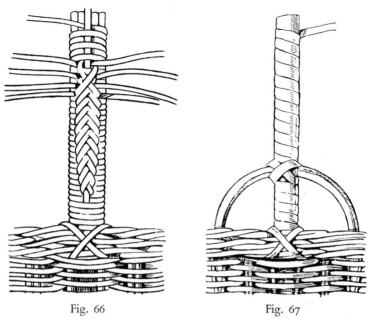

Fig. 66   Fig. 67

the herringbone pattern. Four narrow wrapping canes, prefer-
ably No. 4 chair-seating cane, measuring four times the length
of the handle, are required. These are inserted under the first
four visible sections of the No. 10 cane, one in each with the
wrong side of the cane uppermost, using a bodkin to make way
for them. The canes are drawn through for half their length.
Point all of these at either end. Take the first cane on the left
side, bend this over and thread it under the fifth section of the
No. 10 cane on the right-hand side. Then in a similar way take
the first cane on the right and thread this from the left in the
same space, but under the previous cane. The second cane will
be threaded in the sixth section and so on, forming the pattern
shown. The ends are neatly secured under the herringboning
when complete.

Fig. 67. WRAPPED HANDLE, SUITABLE FOR SMALL HAND
BASKETS. Take a single cane about 8 mm. or 9 mm., and insert
it down the centre of each side of the basket, and secure it in the
same way as Fig. 66. Then insert a smaller size cane in the border,

E

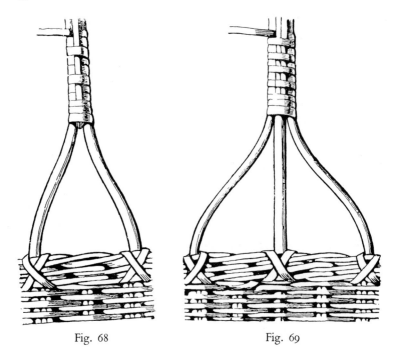

Fig. 68   Fig. 69

about 1½ in. on each side of the handle, bending it to form a semicircle. The end of this should also be pegged. It is fastened to the handle with the wrapping cane during the wrapping of the handle as shown.

Fig. 68. WRAPPED HANDLE FOR HAND BASKETS, ETC. Insert two canes of the same length, about 8 mm. in thickness, 2½ in. apart on each side of the basket, carefully measuring the top edge of the basket to obtain the correct position. Draw the two canes together at the top for about 5 in. or 6 in., and secure them with ½ in. thin wire nails. This distance is then wrapped in the same way as the wrapping in Fig. 66, introducing a length of No. 10 cane, but here wrapping twice under and over this alternately instead of once.

Fig. 69. WRAPPED HANDLE FOR HAND BASKETS, ETC. This is very similar to Fig. 68, but here an extra cane is inserted

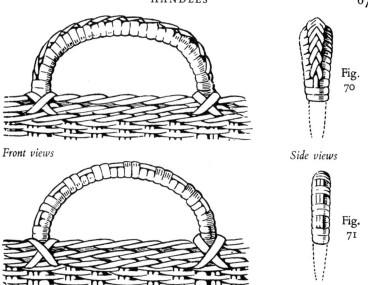

Front views   *Side views*

Fig. 70

Fig. 71

at the centre, making three altogether, which gives additional strength for a large basket. The two side canes are inserted 2 in. from each side of the centre one. Two lengths of No. 10 cane are introduced in the wrapping instead of one.

Fig. 70. SMALL WRAPPED HANDLE, HERRINGBONE PATTERN, FOR HAND BASKETS. Bend over a length of 8 mm. cane with a length of No. 12 cane on each side, making the handle about $3\frac{1}{2}$ in. wide and $1\frac{1}{2}$ in. high. Use the same method of wrapping and working the herringbone pattern as in handle, Fig. 66.

Fig. 71. SMALL WRAPPED HANDLE FOR WORK BASKETS, ETC. A length of 8 mm. cane is used only for the foundation of the handle, which is similar in size and shape to Fig. 70. When wrapping the handle, introduce a length of split cane, enamelled or plain, or two No. 4 canes and arrange the wrapping to go under and over these. Begin and finish the wrapping with a cross in front of the border as previously described.

Fig. 72. SMALL WRAPPED HANDLE. This is similar in size and shape to Fig. 71, and is wrapped in the ordinary way.

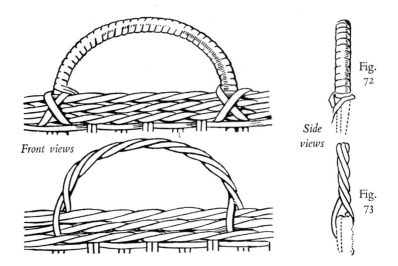

Front views

Side views

Fig. 72

Fig. 73

Fig. 73. SMALL TWISTED HANDLE. Insert a length of No. 6 or thicker cane under the border. Twist the two ends of cane together to make the size of handle required, and then pass these under the border one from each side of the basket. Secure one of the ends by threading it along the weaving. The other is passed round the handle again, carefully following the twist and then secured in the same way, so that there are three canes forming the finished twist.

Fig. 74. TWISTED RING. This is made in a similar way. Tie a length of No. 9 cane into a loop about the size of the ring required as though making a knot. Thread one of the canes over and over the loop, getting an equal twist on both canes. There should be five twists to each ring. Then thread the other end of cane round the ring, following the twist of the first two canes, and cut off the ends. The ring is secured to the basket with a small twisted loop and allowed to hang quite loosely.

Fig. 75. AN ENDLESS PLAITED RING (Small Drop Handle). Take one end of a length of No. 6 cane in the left hand with the short end pointing towards you. Now with the right hand, coil two rings about the size required for the finished ring, side by side and away from you.

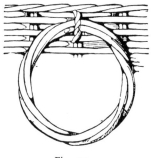 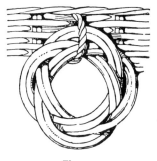

Fig. 74   Fig. 75

We will call the right-hand ring A, and the left B, and they will not change their name no matter what their position may be during the making of the ring.

With the finger and thumb of the left hand hold the ring in that position until you have been once round the ring. Take the long end in the right hand and pass it over A and under B and out to the left-hand side of the ring. Now cross A over B and again pass the cane over A and under B, this time out to the right; over A and under B once more and out to the left. Let the end that forms the start of the ring go loose and take one more stroke with the long cane through the place where the short end starts and out to the right. The edges of the ring must now be pressed inwards and flattened so that it takes the form seen in the illustration. It will be noticed, however, that as yet the twisted ring is made only of single cane, whereas in the illustration double cane appears. With the long remaining end, therefore, thread in and out of the ring, on the inside of the canes, carefully following the first cane until the ring is double throughout, after which the ends are cut off close to the ring. This is also secured to the basket with a small twisted loop.

Fig. 76. SMALL PLAITED HANDLE. To make the nine canes necessary for the plait take three long canes and thread these under the border, drawing them through for half the length, to make six canes. The other three canes are inserted down the centre of the border. The plaiting is then worked to the required

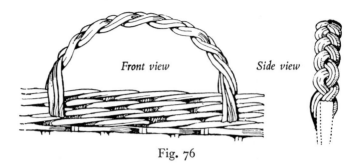

Front view   *Side view*

Fig. 76

length, keeping the canes side by side and flat on the surface as in handle, Fig. 64. When complete point all the ends about 6 in. from the finishing point. These must be attached to the border to correspond with the beginning. Three are inserted down the centre of the border and the remaining six are threaded under the border, three from the outside and three from the inside of the basket, and the ends secured by threading them along the weaving.

Fig. 77. The lower basket (on opposite page) was made from instructions in a book written by an amateur. The cane recommended for the weaving is too large for the stakes, and masters them. The upsetting is too loose and all ends are left too long.

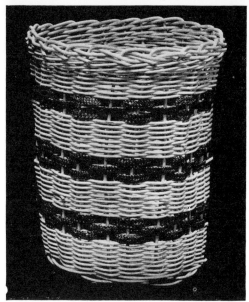

Fig. 77

CHAPTER VII

TRAYS AND BASKETS WITH WOODEN BASES

A teapot stand serves as a useful introduction to canework, for it has a wooden base and requires a minimum amount of work to complete it, but at the same time introduces the working of a foot border, upsetting and finishing border. Actually it is the same as the working of a tray on a miniature scale, so that after the stand a tray can be more easily made.

A round stand is the simplest, as there are no corners to manipulate.

ROUND TEAPOT STAND (Fig. 78)

Materials required: Wooden base, 7 in. diameter; 1 oz. of No. 6 cane for stakes; $\frac{1}{2}$ oz. of No. 3 cane for weaving.

Cut sufficient stakes $7\frac{1}{2}$ in. long and insert them through the holes of the base for $3\frac{1}{2}$ in. ready to work a foot border on the underside, and while doing so let the edge of the base rest on a table to keep it in an upright position until all the stakes are inserted and the foot border worked, as otherwise they will be liable to slip out.

FOOT BORDER. The foot border is worked first. Beginning at the nearest edge with the $3\frac{1}{2}$ in. portion of the stakes pointing away from the worker, bend a stake down and pass it behind the next stake and before two others, leaving the end on the inside. Treat the second stake in the same manner as the first, and continue in this way until there are only three stakes left standing upright. These must be woven into the first three stakes of the border, which are eased up to allow for this, carefully following the pattern to make an invisible join. When this has been done, pull the stakes from the top side of the base to tighten the border and to make it even.

WEAVING. For the working of the top side the base is rested flat on a table. Work two rows of three-rod upsetting with the No. 2 cane as described on page 39, and then work a three-rod plain border with the stakes (see Fig. 34, page 50).

SQUARE TEAPOT STAND (Fig. 78)

A 7 in. square wooden base is used with the same quantity of cane as above. Stakes $9\frac{1}{2}$ in. long.

The working of the foot border and upsetting are the same as in the round stand, but the square stand introduces the working of corners. It will be as well to mention here that square bases should be bored with a hole on each side of the corner instead of one in the corner itself, as this makes it much firmer.

Here a three-rod plain border with a follow-on trac is used (Fig. 59, page 60). It is continued round the corners in the ordinary manner except that a little extra care is given to the placing of the canes to make a good corner.

TRAYS (Fig. 78)

Approximate quantity of materials required for various sized trays:

ROUND TRAY

10 in.: 3 oz. No. 5 cane for stakes. $1\frac{1}{2}$ oz. No. 3 cane for weaving
12 in.: 4 oz.   ,,   ,,   2 oz.   ,,   ,,
14 in.: 5 oz.   ,,   ,, $2\frac{1}{2}$ oz.   ,,   ,,

OBLONG OR OVAL TRAY

16 in. by 9 in.: 4 oz. No. 5, 2 oz. No. 3
18 in. by 10 in.: 5 oz.   ,, $2\frac{1}{2}$ oz.   ,,
20 in. by 12 in.: 6 oz.   ,,   3 oz.   ,,
22 in. by 14 in.: 7 oz.   ,, $3\frac{1}{2}$ oz.   ,,

OVAL TRAY

Cut sufficient stakes 14 in. long of No. 5 cane and insert them through the holes of the base for $3\frac{1}{2}$ in. for working the foot border, which is the same as for the teapot stands.

For the top side of the tray work four rows of three-rod upsetting with No. 3 cane (see Fig. 17, page 39). When complete, work a two-rod three-stroke plaited border (page 52). This border is especially suitable for trays as it gives a firm broad rim, but any of the other borders mentioned as being suitable can be substituted if preferred.

OBLONG TRAY

This is similar to the oval tray, but shows how a practical and

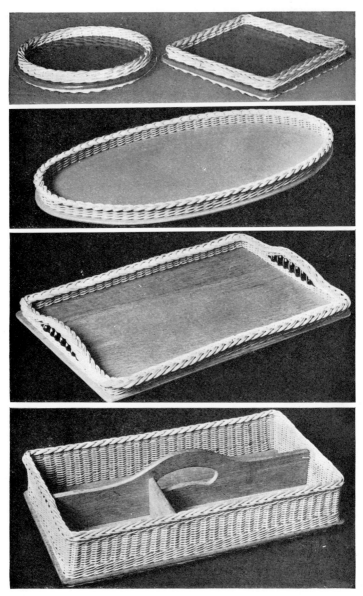

Fig. 78. ROUND AND SQUARE TEAPOT STANDS, OVAL TRAY,
OBLONG TRAY AND KNIFE BASKET

effective handle may be worked on the ends of a tray in the process of weaving by threading four, five or six wooden beads, one for each stake according to the size of the tray, on to the centre stakes of each end. Two rows of three-rod upsetting are worked before adding the beads, after which two more rows are worked resting on the top of the beads at each end to form the handle shape. A two-rod five-stroke plaited border (page 55) is the most suitable in this case, as it has a broader flange for gripping, but the stakes should be 16 in. long.

A TRAY WITH A GLASS TOP

The glass is held in position by the weaving of the side of the tray, so that its size must be carefully considered. The edge of the glass should be just far enough away from the stakes to allow a No. 3 cane to lie between them (see Fig. 79).

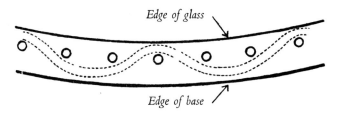

Fig. 79. TRAY WITH GLASS TOP

Work one row of three-rod upsetting first, and cut off the ends of the cane. Lay the glass in position on the base. The top of the glass should be level with the upsetting so that the next row of weaving will rest on it and hold it firmly in position. Work a row of five-rod waling, as this will come well over the edge of the glass. Start with five canes and pass the left-hand cane each time in front of two stakes and behind three. Thread the ends through and cut them off to complete the row. Then proceed with three-rod waling in the ordinary way.

KNIFE BASKET (Fig. 78)

Materials required: A wooden base 18 in. by 10 in., and two wooden partitions, one being shaped to form a handle, 6 oz. No. 8 cane for stakes, 6 oz. No. 3 cane for weaving.

This basket is a development of the rectangular tray.

Cut sufficient stakes 13 in. long and insert them in the base. Work a foot border on the underside behind one stake and in front of two. On the top side work four rows of three-rod upsetting, $1\frac{1}{2}$ in. of randing and two rows of waling. Before starting to rand insert an extra stake on the right-hand side of each of the two corner stakes. This is to strengthen the corners during the working. Short pieces will do as they will have to be cut off quite close before bordering. Work a three-rod plain border with a follow-on trac (Fig. 59, page 60).

Place the partitions in the basket and secure them with $\frac{3}{4}$ in. nails driven through the base. Attach the ends to the basket by passing a length of twisted No. 3 cane through a hole in the partition and round a stake, threading the ends away in the weaving.

ROUND WORK BASKET (Fig. 80)
Materials required: Round base 8 in., approximately 6 oz. No. 6 cane for stakes, 4 oz. No. 3 cane, and two lengths enamelled cane for weaving.

Cut sufficient stakes 14 in. long of No. 6 cane for an 8 in. wooden base, of which the holes are $\frac{1}{2}$ in. to $\frac{5}{8}$ in. apart. Insert these and work the foot border as in the tray.

WEAVING. Before starting to weave, peg the base on to a workboard, as previously mentioned in 'Hints for the Worker', so that it turns round easily. Work four rows of three-rod upsetting with No. 3 cane, and arrange for this basket to have an even number of stakes (see page 104). At this stage insert a bye-stake by the side of each stake, after which work $3\frac{1}{2}$ in. of randing with the No. 3 cane, starting at the finishing point of the upsetting and using each of the double stakes as one stake. Press the stakes slightly outwards during the weaving as there will be a tendency for them to be drawn inwards. When the $3\frac{1}{2}$ in. has been completed, add two rows of waling and then introduce any of the bands of pattern weaving shown in the Sampler Paper Basket (Fig. 27, page 46).

Above this work two rows of waling before bordering.

Fig. 80. ROUND WORK BASKET AND WASTE PAPER BASKET

A trac border is used here. Each double stake, in turn, is bent down 1 in. above the waling and passed in front of two stakes, behind one and in front of one. If desired, any of the following trac borders can be used instead: Figs. 31, 32, 33, 35, pages 49-51.

WASTE PAPER BASKET (Fig. 80)

Materials required: Round 3-ply base 8 in., approximately 7 oz. No. 6 cane for stakes, 8 oz. No. 4 cane and 2 oz. pulp wrapping cane for weaving.

The waste paper basket shown can be made in a similar way to the work basket, but is taller, with the sides gradually sloping out so that the top measures 10 in. in diameter before bordering. The stakes must be 23 in. long of No. 6 cane. The foot border is worked first, and then four rows of three-rod upsetting with No. 4 cane, after which bye-stakes are inserted, making them the same length as the main stakes. Now rand to a depth of 5 in. from the base and work two rows of waling; then, to give variation and interest to the basket, work a few rows of randing with flat wrapping cane or enamelled cane. If preferred, any of the following could be introduced: slewing, double cane chain pairing or chain waling with single or double canes. Add two more rows of waling with ordinary cane and continue randing to a depth of 8½ in. from the base. Three more rows of waling

are worked before the border, but during the working of these
rows the main stakes and bye-stakes are separated and each used
as one stake, otherwise the stakes would be too far apart to give
a firm border, as the distance between them is considerably
greater than at the beginning owing to the sloping sides. This,
of course, would not be necessary should it be decided to make
a basket with upright sides. The border suggested for this basket
is the three-rod plain border, with the back trac as described in
border, Fig. 35, page 52, but a plaited border could be used
instead, if preferred (see page 56).

OVAL WORK BASKET (Fig. 81)

Materials required: An oval wooden base 12 in. by 8 in.; approximately $\frac{1}{2}$ lb. No. 6 cane for stakes; 3 oz. No. 3 cane for upsetting
and waling; 4 oz. No. 2 cane for randing, and 54 oval wooden
beads.

The sides of the basket slope out a little, measuring 4 in. deep
on the inside.

Cut sufficient stakes 17 in. long and insert them in the base.
Work a foot border on the underside, Fig. 58, page 60.

On the top side work three rows of upsetting with the No. 3
cane, and then rand to a depth of 3 in. from the base with the
No. 2 cane. Add two rows of waling with the No. 3 cane before
working a band of fitching as described in Fig. 23, page 43. This
basket shows the introduction of beads in the fitching, these
being threaded on each of the main stakes.

Cut sufficient bye-stakes 6 in. long from the No. 3 cane to
insert on both sides of each stake. Add a cane to the two canes
used for working the fitching and work a row of waling before
adding the border. This is a combination of the three-rod plain
border, page 50, and the single-trac border, page 48. The three-
rod plain border is worked first and then the trac border with
the ends protruding on the outside, making a broad flat rim to
the basket.

*When a wooden base has an odd number of holes and an even number
is required for the basket being made, proceed as follows: after the first
two rows of upsetting, bye-stake one of the stakes and divide them with
the next two rows of upsetting.*

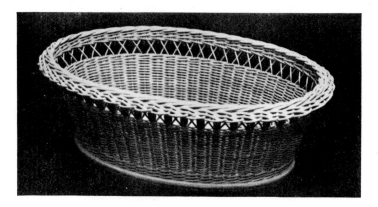

Fig. 81. OVAL WORK BASKET

CHEESE BOX HOLDER (Fig. 82)

Materials required: $5\frac{1}{2}$ in. thin round wooden base, made for the purpose with a large hole in the centre so that the box can easily be removed, and with 31 small holes for stakes; $\frac{1}{2}$ oz. No. 3 cane for stakes, $5\frac{1}{2}$ in. long; 2 pieces No. 1 cane for pairing, 36 in. long; 1 piece No. 3 cane for working in the handle, 36 in. long; 2 pieces No. 12 cane, 14 in. long, for the handle.

The foot border is worked behind one, in front of one, leaving the end inside. The sides can be worked on a flat table. Work four rows of pairing. The sides are to be upright to ensure a good fit for the box.

The top border is a trac—in front of one, behind one, in front of one, and leave the end inside. It is now ready for the handle. Make points on the four ends of the two pieces 14 in. long, insert two of the ends on the left-hand side of the two stakes with one stake between, so that they will be about 1 in. apart. Now bring the two canes together about 2 in. above the top edge of the basket, and twist one over the other alternately eight times. Then bend them over to form the handle, and insert the ends.

To give the handle additional strength, take the piece of No. 3 cane 36 in. long, squeeze it in the centre, and insert the end between the top rows of pairing and in between the two handle

Fig. 82. CHEESE BOX HOLDER

canes. Give the doubled cane three short twists before taking it over the handle. Work the canes separately so that each cane lies in a separate twist of the handle. Match the opposite side with the small twists and thread the ends backwards and forwards to make them secure.

TOAST RACK (Fig. 83)

Materials required: A wooden base $5\frac{3}{4}$ in. by $3\frac{1}{2}$ in.; four pieces of 5 mm. cane 8 in. long for the divisions, and two pieces 12 in. long for the handle; one-and-a-half lengths of orange and half a length black enamelled cane; four black wooden beads for feet; a few $\frac{1}{2}$ in. and $\frac{3}{4}$ in. nails.

The base has six holes along each side. The centre two on each side are used for the handle.

After damping the canes, bend one of the short pieces into an arch shape and insert the ends in the two end holes on opposite sides of the base, making them flush with the underside. Secure them by driving a $\frac{1}{2}$ in. nail through the edge of the base, cutting off the head of the nail before finally driving it in. If the cane is too large for the holes, pare down the ends very slightly to make a tight fit.

Insert the other short pieces in the same way and then the two handle canes in the two centre pairs of holes. These are brought together at the centre, and after being secured with a nail are

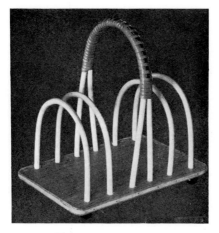

Fig. 83. TOAST RACK

wrapped together across the top for 6 in. with orange enamelled cane, laying a length of the black on the handle and wrapping under and over it in the manner described in the handle, Fig. 69, on page 66.

The ends of the orange cane are secured by threading under the last wraps and down again under the last two on the under-side of the handle.

Fill up the holes in the beads with cane and then fix one at each corner on the underside of the base with a ¾ in. nail, which is driven up through the cane in the end holes.

OVAL NURSERY BASKET (Fig. 84)

This basket and the oblong nursery basket which follows are both direct developments of an oval and an oblong tray.

It should be noted that the sides of this basket slope outwards slightly, the depth of the inside being approximately 4½ in. when complete.

Materials required: An oval wooden base 18 in. by 10 in.; approximately 10 oz. No. 8 cane for stakes; 10 oz. No. 5 cane for bye-stakes, upsetting, waling and fitching; 2 oz. No. 3 cane for randing.

Cut sufficient No. 8 stakes for the base 22 in. long, and twice the number of No. 5 bye-stakes 6 in. long.

F

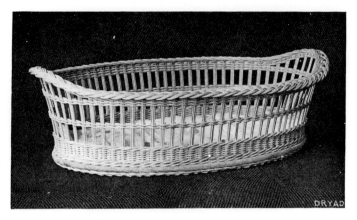

Fig. 84. OVAL NURSERY BASKET

Work a foot border on the underside of the base as for a tray, then on the top side work two rows of upsetting with the No. 5 cane, followed by 1 in. of randing with No. 3 cane. Next insert a bye-stake on both sides of each of the main stakes, after which work one row of waling with the No. 5 cane. Work the band of fitching as described in Fig. 24, page 44, allowing a space of 1⅛ in. between the rows of fitching.

After working the second two rows of pairing or fitching, another row is worked, close to the previous two along the sides, but gradually raising up at each end to form the handle shape shown in the illustration. Beyond this work a row of waling by adding another cane to make the necessary three.

Cut off the ends of the bye-stakes level with the last row and then work a two-rod five-stroke plaited border.

OBLONG NURSERY BASKET (Fig. 85)

Materials required: An oblong wooden base 18 in. by 10 in.; ¾ lb. No. 8 cane for stakes; approximately ¾ lb. No. 5 for bye-stakes, upsetting, waling, and fitching; 2 oz. No. 3 for randing. Also two pieces 13 in. long of 8 mm. cane for the handles; four pieces of 8 mm. 6 in. long (for temporary use); a long length of pulp wrapping cane for handles.

The working of this basket is the same as the oval basket as

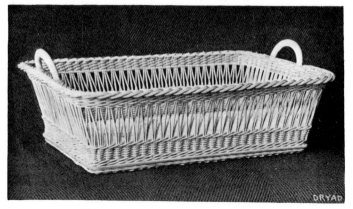

Fig. 85. OBLONG NURSERY BASKET

far as the end of the randing. Now point and insert the four short 8 mm. canes in the ends of the basket where the handles will come. These should be about 4 in. apart and inserted to the left of the stake.

Now put in the No. 5 bye-stakes, one on each side of the main stakes, to make the cross fitch, but arrange the bye-stakes in the ends of the basket so that the cross is omitted on each side of the 8 mm. canes. The 8 mm. cane and stake by its side are treated as one. The stake will be required in this position to work the border, after which the 8 mm. canes will be pulled out and the proper handle inserted.

Now work the three-rod wale on the top of the randing, and when putting on the fitch the stake by the side of each 8 mm. cane will be carried straight up, not crossed over. If so desired it can be cut out after the border is completed.

For the band of fitching, which is worked as described in Fig. 23 on page 43, measure up a height of $3\frac{3}{4}$ in. above the base on the inside of the basket. Add another cane to the two canes used for the fitching and work four rows of waling.

Cut off the bye-stakes level with the top of the last row and work a two-rod five-stroke plaited border, the start of which should be in the side of the basket. The handle canes are then shaped and inserted in place of the four 8 mm. canes, being secured in either of the ways mentioned in the handle, Fig. 72, on page 68, and wrapped with wrapping cane.

Here again the sides of the basket slope outwards a little.

LEMONADE TRAY BASKET (Fig. 86)

Materials required: 14 in. round wooden base bored at the edge and again with a 6 in. circle of holes at the centre for the inside basket which holds the jug; 6 oz. No. 7 cane for stakes, 6 oz. No. 3 cane for weaving, and six lengths of enamelled cane, two lengths 8 mm. cane 35 in. long for the handle, and eight more pieces 3⅛ in. long for the divisions, with eight pieces of No. 5 seating cane 4 ft. long for wrapping them.

The inside jug basket is worked first. Cut sufficient stakes 9 in. long and insert them in the base and work a foot border on the underside, passing each cane in front of two stakes, leaving the ends inside. Work two rows of three-rod upsetting and then rand to a depth of 2 in. Work two rows of waling and then work a three-rod plain border, Fig. 34, page 52.

The handle canes are bent into shape and inserted next, but they are not joined together at the top until the outer basket is completed. The ends of the handle are each held in position by driving a ¾ in. nail through the edge of the base, cutting off the head of the nail before finally driving it in.

Cut sufficient stakes 13 in. long for the outer basket and the same number of bye-stakes 3½ in. long. Insert the stakes in the base. Work a foot border behind one and in front of two stakes. Work two rows of three-rod upsetting and then insert the bye-stakes on the right-hand side of the stakes. Work 1 in. of randing and two rows of waling, after which add one row of enamelled cane, one row of ordinary cane, and another of enamelled cane. Work two more rows of waling and then cut off the bye-stakes level with the top of the last one. Before bordering it is necessary to insert a stake by the right-hand side of each of the handle canes, making them the same height as the others. A three-rod plain border with a follow-on trac, Fig. 59, page 60, is used.

The handle canes are now drawn together 9 in. from the base at each side and nailed together. They are wrapped with the enamelled cane, being secured with a cross, as described in handle,

Fig. 86. LEMONADE TRAY BASKET

Fig. 66, page 64. In wrapping over the double portion of th
handle three lengths of the No. 3 cane are placed along the top
and the enamelled cane is wrapped twice under and over them
alternately.

The final stage is to insert the eight short canes between the
small inside basket and the larger outer one to form the divisions
for the glasses. Divide the edge of both baskets into eight equal
parts and place the ends of the canes to these points just below
the border, temporarily fixing them with nails passed through
the sides of the basket. They are finally secured with a length
of seating cane as follows. Secure the end of the cane to the small
inside basket by threading it through the weaving below the two
rows of waling, bringing it out on the inside. Pass it back through
the basket above the waling and lay it along the top of the 8 mm.

cane. Thread it through the outer basket above the waling and back again below it. Pass it along the underneath of the 8 mm. cane and repeat once more from the beginning so that it passes twice above and below the 8 mm. cane, thus making two short stitches over the waling in both baskets. Then proceed to wrap the cane securing the end of the seating cane by threading it away in the weaving.

ROUND FRUIT BASKET (Fig. 87)

Materials required: Round base 5 in., approximately 4 oz. of No. 6 cane for stakes, 4 oz. of No. 3 cane for weaving.

Cut sufficient stakes 18 in. long and insert them into the base.

When the foot border has been worked, behind one and in front of two, and completed, squeeze all the stakes level with the top side of the base. Bend each one down to the left and pass it behind two stakes, threading the last one through to complete. The stakes will now stand out as flat as the base. This is essential when using a wooden base for making a basket with curved sides, in order to obtain the necessary curve.

Now add a bye-stake to each of the stakes, letting the ends of these project on the wooden base about 1 in. These ends will afterwards be cut off.

Work two rows of pairing with the No. 3 cane, dividing all the stakes into single ones while doing so, still keeping the basket on a flat surface. Without these extra stakes it would be found that when the widest part of the basket is reached the stakes would be much too far apart for the work to be firm.

The pairing is started on the far side of the basket. When the two rows are complete, finish off the ends and peg the base on to a workboard resting on the floor and knees so that the stakes appear in a vertical position and straightforward for working.

Now work two rows of three-rod upsetting. Then shape the stakes to the desired curve. Rand to a depth of $3\frac{1}{2}$ in., taking care to keep the stakes curved.

Two rows of waling are now worked before adding a three-rod three-stroke plaited border (see Fig. 46, page 55).

The top should measure about 9 in. in diameter when the basket is complete.

Fig. 87. ROUND FRUIT BASKET AND BOWL-SHAPED BASKET

BOWL-SHAPED BASKET (Fig. 87)

Materials required: Round base 5 in.; 4 oz. No. 3 cane; 4 oz. No. 6 cane; 2 lengths enamelled cane.

A 5 in. base with 25 holes is used again, and the basket is started in exactly the same way. The shaping of the stakes must be carefully done as here the sides are much fuller. The top should measure 9 in. in diameter when the basket is complete.

Rand to a depth of $3\frac{1}{2}$ in. and then add one row of waling with No. 6 cane. Coloured cane is introduced at this stage. In the basket illustrated there are three rows of enamelled cane all passing under and over the same stakes, but any of the bands of weaving shown in the sampler basket on page 46 could be used. Two rows of waling using the No. 6 cane again are worked before the trac border, in which the stakes are taken in front of two, behind one, and in front of one, leaving the end inside. Two twisted rings, as described in handle, Fig. 74, page 69, are fastened to the sides of the basket underneath the first row of waling with two small loops of twisted cane.

CORNER LINEN BASKET (Fig. 88)

Approximate quantity of materials required: $1\frac{1}{2}$ lb. No. 12 cane; 1 lb. No. 5 cane; 14 ft. 8 mm. split cane for beading; $\frac{1}{2}$ lb. No. 9 cane; $1\frac{1}{2}$ lb. pulp wrapping cane; packet of mixed wire nails.

The three sticks provided with the various pieces of the frame should be fitted into the three large holes in the base, the end that has a part cut away, making a small ledge, being uppermost with the ledge facing inwards. The smaller of the triangular

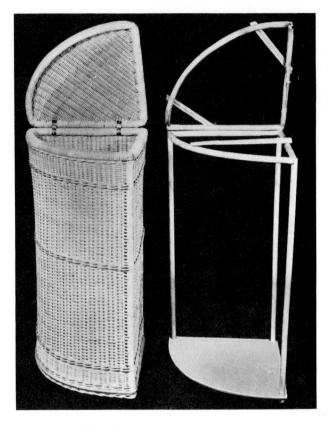

Fig. 88. CORNER LINEN BASKET

shaped frames is placed inside the sticks and nailed in position resting on the ledge. The larger of the two frames is for the lid.

Cut the required number of stakes 30 in. long of No. 12 cane, and an equal number 24 in. long for the bye-stakes. Insert the stakes in the holes in the base to project 6 in. on the underside, and work one row of three-rod upsetting. Finish with a border made by working behind one and in front of two.

The body part of the basket is now started with two rows of upsetting worked with No. 9 cane. Above this work 1½ in. of randing with No. 5 cane, two rows of waling with No. 9 cane,

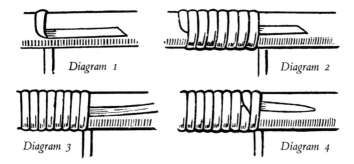

Fig. 89

and then 10 in. of randing using pulp wrapping cane. After the randing work two more rows of waling with No. 9 cane and another 8 in. of randing with wrapping cane, then two more rows of waling and $1\frac{3}{4}$ in. of randing with No. 5 cane, leaving about $\frac{1}{4}$ in. space below the top of the frame.

The stakes are now nailed to the frame and two rows of beading of 8 mm. split cane are added, and the ends of all the stakes cut off neatly, level with the top. The top of the basket is now ready to be wrapped, and this is done as follows. The wrapping is worked from left to right and away from the worker, and the lines of wrapping must be kept upright and quite close together.

Diagrams 1 and 2 in Fig. 89 show the method of commencing the wrapping. Lay the end of cane along the frame with the right side next to the frame, choosing the least conspicuous place. Secure this with a $\frac{1}{4}$ in. nail, and then bend over the length of cane into position for starting the wrapping as shown.

The finishing of the cane should be arranged in the least conspicuous place as with the beginning. To secure the end thread it under the last loop of the wrapping, pull it tight and put a $\frac{1}{4}$ in. nail through both canes. Then cut off the end of the cane quite close to the wrapping.

When about 10 in. only of cane remains, lay a new length of cane along the under side of the frame with the right side nearest to it. Continue wrapping with the old length of cane, taking it over the new cane until only about 2 in. remains (see Diagram

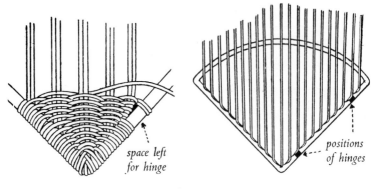

Fig. 90

3). Now take hold of both the old and the new canes close to the frame and twist them over to the right, thus reversing the position of the canes (see Diagram 4). Then proceed with the wrapping in the ordinary way, using the new cane. The joining point should afterwards be tapped with a hammer to make it quite flat.

When the wrapping is complete, work one row of waling in the space under the edge of the frame.

To work the lid, take the remaining triangular shaped frame and, starting with one stake at the middle corner, cover the corner as neatly as possible with the weaving (see Fig. 90). As the frame widens, add new stakes on either side, binding them to the frame with the weaving, which is wrapped twice round the frame at the end of each row. As each stake is covered with two or three rows of randing a bye-stake is inserted by the side of it.

At the places marked in Fig. 90, leave a space for the hinges about $\frac{3}{4}$ in. wide. This is done by working round a stake instead of round the frame.

When the weaving is finished, squeeze all the stakes with the round-nosed pliers, bend them over and nail them to the curved side of the frame. A split beading cane is then nailed over the ends and the frame wrapped with wrapping cane. Work one row of pairing to fill the space made by the wrapping.

Fig. 91. OVAL FRUIT BASKET

The lid is hinged to the basket with two thin copper bands which require to be 6 in. long and ½ in. wide. Bore a hole in each band ⅜ in. from the end, to take a No. 6 round-headed screw. Screw the bands to the top rail of the basket to correspond with the slots in the lid. Now pass the other ends through the lid slots and pull, and hammer them tight with the lid in a raised position. Now bore a hole in the copper bands to come into position on the inside of the top rail and screw on. Cut off surplus ends and tap down with a hammer. Dent the copper bands inside and out with the hammer, just where the lid touches the basket. This holds the lid in the correct position.

OVAL FRUIT BASKET WITH ONE-ROD FIVE-STROKE PLAITED BORDER (Fig. 91)

Materials required: Oval base, 9 in. by 5 in.; 2 oz. No. 5 cane for stakes; 1 oz. No. 1 cane for weaving; 1 length double-sided enamelled cane for introduction of colour; 1 piece of 8 mm. cane for handle, 28 in. long; 2 pieces of 8 mm. cane 12 in. long for handle supports.

Cut the stakes 13 in. long. Insert in the base and border as for a tray on a workboard and allow to turn freely.

Work four rows of upsetting with the No. 1 cane, holding the stakes well out and the weaving close down while working to set the stakes before starting to rand. Before doing this it is advisable to add two more stakes at each end or the stakes would be too wide apart at the border.

Work to a depth of $1\frac{1}{4}$ in. above the upset, then begin the building up of the sloping ends by turning back with the cane near the middle of the side. On arriving opposite to the turning point, work to the right this time again, and turn back at the stake next to the one first used. Continue thus until all the stakes belonging to that end of the basket are used. Treat the other end in a similar manner.

Above this, work two rows of waling, and then two rows of enamelled cane with a round cane worked in between. Then work three rows of waling.

Before bordering, insert pegs to receive the handle (see page 96). Instructions for doing the border will be found on page 58.

When a wooden base has an odd number of holes and an even number is required for the basket being made, proceed as follows. After the first two rows of upsetting, bye-stake one of the stakes and divide them with the next two rows of upsetting.

PICNIC BASKET No. 1, TO HOLD TWO THERMOS FLASKS AND LUNCH TIN (Fig. 92)

Materials required: Wooden base, 16 in. by $4\frac{1}{2}$ in., with 64 holes; $\frac{1}{2}$ lb. No. 6 cane for stakes; 5 oz. No. 3 cane for weaving; 2 lengths of enamelled cane for introduction of colour; 5 lengths of narrow enamelled cane for wrapping; 2 pieces of 8 mm. cane 24 in. long for handles; 2 oz. pulp wrapping cane for weaving.

Cut 64 pieces of No. 6 cane 15 in. long, and 64 pieces 12 in. long, for stakes. Insert them in the base and border as for a tray, that is, behind one and in front of two, leaving the ends at the back. Before starting to weave, it should, of course, be pegged on to a workboard to facilitate the working and shaping.

Work four rows of three-rod upsetting, then bye-stake and rand with pulp wrapping cane and No. 3 cane alternately. This

Fig. 92. PICNIC BASKET NO. I

makes the basket more rigid than if worked with the flat cane only. Work for 4 in. above the upsetting; then two rows of chain waling followed by two rows of the enamelled cane with a round cane worked in between; then four rows of chain waling and repeat the colour pattern, ending with two rows of chain waling.

The stakes should be well damped and allowed to rest a few minutes before bordering, and provision should be made to receive the handles by having four pieces of 8 mm. cane about 7 in. long pointed and inserted well down the sides of the basket at the places where the handles are to be. These are removed when the handles are inserted. Otherwise the handles can be shaped, pointed and inserted before starting the border. Wrap

Fig. 93. PICNIC BASKET NO. 2

and secure in the usual way (see page 68). Any of the borders, Figs. 31, 32 or 33 on pages 49 and 50 may be adopted.

Care should be taken to keep the ends of the basket upright.

When a wooden base has an odd number of holes and an even number is required for the basket being made, proceed as follows. After the first two rows of upsetting, bye-stake one of the stakes and divide them with the next two rows of upsetting.

PICNIC BASKET No. 2 (Fig. 93)

Designed for those who desire to work with one weaving cane. *Materials required:* Wooden base, 16 in. by $4\frac{1}{2}$ in., with 63 holes; $\frac{1}{2}$ lb. No. 6 cane for stakes; $\frac{1}{2}$ lb. No. 3 cane and $\frac{1}{4}$ lb. pulp wrapping cane for weaving sides; 2 pieces 8 mm. cane, 24 in. in length, for handle; 4 pieces, 7 in. in length, for inserting into the basket to make provision for the handle to be pushed in later, and a further 4 pieces, 7 in. in length, if No. 2 handle is used.

Cut 63 pieces of No. 6 cane for stakes and 63 pieces for bye-stakes. These will be 18 in. and 10 in. respectively. Take the long ones and insert through the base, and put on the foot trac, then four rows of three-rod upsetting. Sharpen the bye-stakes and push in one to each main stake. Put on 1 in. of randing with No. 3 cane, followed by a three-rod wale. Thin off for about 3 in. the end of a piece of wrapping cane to give a gradual start, and put on 4 in., followed by a chain wale. Be sure the work is level.

Sharpen four of the 7 in. lengths of 8 mm. cane and insert into the randing each side about 1½ in., with 5 in. between. This will make provision for the handle when required. Each should be pushed down by the side of a stake and woven in with the stake.

A double chain pair is now worked, followed by a single chain wale. One more double chain pair with four rows of waling complete the sides.

Cut off the short stake of each pair quite close to the top of the waling, and border with a four-rod plain border (page 51). Follow this with a follow-on trac (Fig. 59). Cut off the ends inside the basket long enough for them to lie on a stake, and so prevent them from coming through the front again.

HANDLE. Two types can be used, either an ordinary push-in handle or a hinged one. The former will require two lengths of 8 mm. cane 24 in. in length. Find the middle and mark, also make a mark 8 in. each side of the middle. Bend the cane in the centre to give a handle measuring 5 in. across. Sharpen the ends, remove the dummy canes from the basket, and push down until the 8 in. marks rest on top of the border. Fasten in and wrap in the usual way.

For the hinged handle, take the other four short 8 mm. canes and sharpen for 3 in. to a point. At 4 in. scoop out three-quarters of the cane for the remaining 3 in., thinning off to nothing. The scoop-out should be quite sharp, almost a right-angle cut. Now take something round and just about ⅛ in.

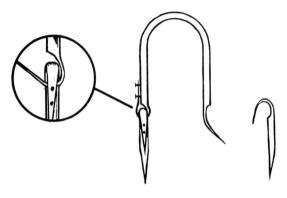

Fig. 94

larger than the 8 mm. cane and place it on top of the scoop-out Bring the thinned-off end over and nail down with $\frac{3}{8}$ in. cane nails. Treat the remaining three in the same way. There are now four eyed and sharpened canes to be inserted where the dummy canes are drawn out. Fasten in the usual way.

Now take the long 8 mm. canes, find the middle and mark, and mark 8 in. each side. Bend the handle as before, but this time scoop out as for the short canes at the 8 in. marks. Thread the ends through the eyes, nail up the handle and wrap. (Fig. 94.)

The eyes of the short canes should look along the border, not across it, and the scoop-out on the handle should be at the side, to allow it to work as a hinge.

The 8 mm. cane used for this handle will work much better if soaked in water for one hour.

CHAPTER VIII

BASKETS WITH CANE BASES

Cane bases are commonly made round, oval, oblong or square, according to the shape of the basket desired. The round and oval bases are somewhat similar in construction, and being simpler to work than the oblong or square bases, are introduced first.

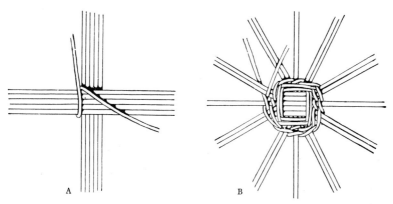

A   B

Fig. 95. SHOWING THE WORKING OF A ROUND BASE

BARREL-SHAPED SHOPPING BASKET (Fig. 97)
Materials required: Approximately 1 oz. No. 12 cane for base stakes; 4 oz. No. 9 cane for side stakes; 2 oz. No. 3 cane, 1 oz. No. 4 cane, 2 lengths enamelled cane for weaving; 1 pair handle canes, and 5 oz. wrapping cane.
ROUND BASE. Ten No. 12 canes, 7 in. long, are required for the base. Split one through the centre with a penknife for a distance of about 1¼ in. and thread another one through the slit. If after inserting the penknife it is turned slightly first to the left and then to the right the cane will split quite easily. Split four more canes in the same way and thread them on to this cane and then insert the remaining four canes through all the split ones,

G

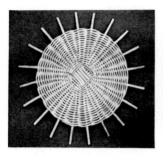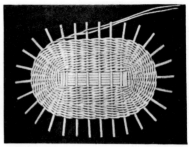

Fig. 96. ROUND AND OVAL CANE BASE

so that there are five canes each way forming a cross, Fig. 95 (A).

The bottom is worked with pairing. Squeeze a length of cane at the centre and bend it in half to make the two canes necessary for this, and place the loop round one of the groups of five canes, Fig. 95 (A). Work two rows round the four groups of five canes, using each group as one cane. After this the five stakes in each group are divided into three, i.e. 2, 1 and 2 stakes, using the two stakes in each case as one and pulling them into position to make the distance between them more equal, Fig. 95 (B). Three rows of pairing are worked and then the stakes are further divided and used singly, taking care now to arrange them at equal distances apart. When the first row has been done bend all the stakes over to make the base slightly curved. Continue the pairing until the bottom measures 5 in. across, taking care to get the rows quite close together, otherwise it will not be firm. Also keep the stakes at equal distances apart. When complete cut the stakes off quite close to the work.

SIDE. Forty 16-in. lengths of No. 9 cane are required for the stakes. Point one end of each of these for about $\frac{3}{4}$ in. Insert them as far as possible into the base, one on either side of each stake, making a hole for them with a bodkin. When this has been done, it will be noticed that although the bottom stakes were cut off quite close to the work, they are now showing about $\frac{1}{8}$ in. beyond the edge. This is due to the pressure in inserting the stakes, and a row of pairing must be worked to cover them, including each stake and the new one inserted on either side as one stake. When the row is complete, secure the ends. The new stakes must now

Fig. 97. BARREL-SHAPED SHOPPING BASKET, AND A BOWL-SHAPED
BASKET WITH A TURNED-IN TOP

be bent up for the sides. Place the bottom of the basket on a
table with the curved side uppermost, and squeeze all the stakes
with round-nosed pliers quite close to the work, then bend
them up at a sharp angle.

The next stage is the upsetting; that is, the first few rows of
work to set the stakes in order at equal distances apart, and also
at the correct angle. The first row must be of four-rod upsetting,
using No. 3 cane, and the base is held firmly between the knees
while working this. When the row is complete cut off one of
the canes and continue working three rows of three-rod upsetting
with the remaining three canes as described on page 39. While
working these just rest the base on the knee, and when complete
cut off the ends on the inside.

Now peg the basket on to a workboard and bend all the stakes
to form the barrel shape, again rather more than is actually
required as they are inclined to straighten during the working.
Begin randing with the flat wrapping cane close to the finishing
ends of the upsetting. As there is an even number of stakes two
lengths must be used. Work to a depth of 6 in., finishing the last

two rows level with the starting-point. Examine the work and make it quite level by tapping it lightly with the rapping iron. Add two rows of waling with the No. 4 cane, and when complete continue the randing with the No. 3 cane for $1\frac{1}{4}$ in. Introduce two rows of coloured enamelled cane and then work two more rows of waling with No. 4 cane to give firmness to the top of the basket, which will then be ready for bordering. The three-rod plain border, Fig. 34, page 50, is used.

The three-rod plain border with the follow-on trac border, Fig. 59, page 60, makes an excellent border for a shopping basket, as there are no ends left on the outside to catch on one's clothes.

HANDLE. Figs. 66, 67, 68 and 69, described on pages 64-66, can be used, but the handle illustrated is Fig. 68.

When this basket has been managed successfully various other shapes with a cane base can be made, but the worker should always aim at a definite shape and never allow the basket to make its own shape, as some are tempted to do.

BOWL-SHAPED SHOPPING BASKET (Fig. 97)
WITH A TURNED-IN TOP

Materials required: 1 oz. No. 12 cane for base stakes; 6 oz. No. 9 cane for side stakes; 6 oz. No. 3 cane, 1 oz. No. 6 cane for weaving; 2 lengths enamelled cane; 1 pair handle canes; 1 oz. of wrapping cane for handle.

A similar base is required to that made for the barrel-shaped basket, and also the same number of stakes of No. 9 cane for the sides, but only 11 in. in length here. These must be made to slope out more in the upsetting than in the previous basket, and after this, shaped according to the illustration. The turn-in at the top is arranged later.

Rand to a depth of 5 in. with No. 3 cane, at which stage the basket should measure $10\frac{1}{2}$ in. across the top. See that the work is quite level, and if not, tap it with a rapping iron. Split cane could be used for the randing if desired. Work two rows of three-rod waling, and when this has been done squeeze all the stakes with the round-nosed pliers and bend them sharply inwards for the top of the basket. A row of four-rod waling is then worked with No. 6 cane to cover the bend and to hold the stakes in position. Complete the row and after this work three rows of pairing with No. 3 cane, taking care to keep all the stakes bending inwards in the correct position and to finish off the ends of the final row level with the beginning. Introduce two rows of enamelled cane, one row of black and one of orange, or any colour desired, worked in the same way as randing, but allow the ends to overlap at the joining points to make them secure. Two rows of waling with dyed pulp cane can be used in place of the enamelled cane if desired. Add one row of waling with No. 6 cane and the basket will be ready for the border.

To border, squeeze all the stakes $\frac{1}{4}$ in. above the row of waling and work them in an ordinary foot border, behind one stake and in front of two, but each time holding the stake well down inside the basket with the left hand before bringing it forward to pass in front of the two stakes. This will make the border close and firm. Thread the ends through to complete the pattern of the row correctly at the finish and leave them inside.

HANDLE. The handle should be about 8 mm. in thickness (as thick as a lead pencil), and two lengths of the cane are required. These are bent into position and inserted into the basket through the four-rod waling about 2 in. apart and pegged as in the previous basket. The two canes are then bound together with wrapping cane, introducing enamelled cane if desired, wrapping three times under and over it alternately as in handle, Fig. 68, page 66.

OVAL SHOPPING BASKET (Fig. 98)

Approximate quantity of materials required: Same amount as for bowl-shaped basket.

OVAL BASE. This is rather more difficult than the round base, although made in a somewhat similar way. No. 12 cane is used for the stakes; ten pieces $5\frac{1}{2}$ in. long and five pieces 9 in. long are required. Split the ten short pieces at the centre and thread them on one of the 9 in. pieces. Then insert the other four 9 in. pieces through the slits. Arrange the ten short pieces across the long pieces as follows. Measure a distance of 3 in. across the centre and place three of the short canes in a group at each end

Fig. 98. OVAL SHOPPING BASKET AND ROUND WORK BASKET WITH LID

of this. The four remaining centre canes are arranged at equal
distances across the 3 in. Now wrap the centre bar with a piece
of chair seating cane or No. 3 pulp cane. This holds the cross
stakes in position and makes the opening out of the stakes very
easy.

The stakes are opened out with pairing, using No. 3 cane.
Squeeze a length of this, bend it in the middle, and pass the loop
round one of the groups of three canes which is used as one
stake in each case for the first two rows. The five canes at each
end are treated as one in the same way. When the two rows are
complete, the canes must be divided to begin filling the spaces
at each end of the four corners of the base. Divide the five at each
end to make a group of two, one and two, also each of the groups
of three canes to make two stakes, the two outer canes for one
stake and the remaining one for the other. Two rows of pairing
are worked with the canes in this position. After this they are
further divided into single canes, one cane for each stake,
arranging them at equal distances apart. At this stage couple
another length of No. 3 cane round a stake behind the two canes
already being worked, but put reverse pairing on with this pair.
Work the two pairs separately, one reverse and one ordinary
pairing, continuously round the base. This will give chain pairing

and will prevent any twist in the base. During the working the stakes should be slightly curved as in the round base. When the base is complete, with an equal number of rows on each side of the centre stakes, draw the ends of pairing canes under the last row and cut off all the stakes close to the edge of the work.

SIDE. No. 9 cane is used for the stakes in the side of the basket and these should be 15 in. long. They are inserted in the base as in the barrel-shaped basket, one on either side of each stake, except for the centre two stakes in each side. These have only one stake, or the stakes in the sides would be too close together. The basket is now continued in exactly the same way as the barrel-shaped basket, working one row of pairing to cover the ends of the bottom stakes before bending up the side stakes to the required angle. Then the rows of upsetting and randing are worked until a depth of $3\frac{1}{2}$ in. is reached. Two rows of waling are then worked and, beyond these, four rows of chain pairing with double canes, so that four canes are necessary for each row instead of two. When the rows are complete two more rows of waling are added. The basket should now measure about 5 in. deep and 12 in. by 8 in. across the top, and is ready for bordering.

BORDER. A three-rod plain border is used here, Fig. 34, but any of the borders suggested as being suitable for shopping baskets could be used.

HANDLE. Fig. 68 is used in the basket illustrated, but this also may be changed for one of the other handles for shopping baskets.

ROUND WORK BASKET WITH LID (Fig. 98)

Materials required: Round base 8 in.; approximately 6 oz. No. 6 cane for stakes; 3 oz. No. 12 cane for the lid stakes; 6 oz. No. 3 cane for weaving, and 2 lengths enamelled cane.

Here the basket has a wooden base, but a cane lid, which is worked in a similar way to the cane base. An 8 in. wooden base is used and the basket should measure $5\frac{3}{4}$ in. deep and $10\frac{1}{2}$ in. across the top when complete. The base should have an even number of holes and two weaving canes used. No. 6 cane is used for the stakes, 15 in. long. The foot border and upsetting are the same as previously described, and when these have been worked, cut bye-stakes $11\frac{1}{2}$ in. long and insert them by the side of the stakes. Rand to a depth of $3\frac{1}{2}$ in. and then work two rows of waling and four rows of randing. Enamelled cane is used for the next two or three rows, and then two rows of waling are worked with No. 6 cane.

When a wooden base has an odd number of holes and an even number is required for the basket being made, proceed as follows. After the first two rows of upsetting, bye-stake one of the stakes and divide them with the next two rows of upsetting.

BORDER AND LEDGE FOR LID. The trac border, Fig. 31, is worked first. When complete the remaining double ends on the inside of the basket are used to make a small ledge for the lid to rest on. It is much more satisfactory to have a lid of this kind fitting in the basket than resting on top. The double canes must first be divided into single canes by working one row of pairing. During the working of this the canes must be brought at right angles to the border so that they are all pointing directly to the centre. This will be found rather difficult for a beginner, but must be done firmly and evenly with all the canes at an equal distance apart. When complete a simple trac border as in the foot border is worked with the canes to finish the ledge.

LID. The basket will measure about 10 in. in diameter on the inside; the lid must therefore measure $9\frac{1}{2}$ in. before bordering, thus allowing $\frac{1}{2}$ in. for the border. Half an inch must always be allowed for the border, no matter what size the lid may be.

Ten pieces of No. 12 cane are required, $11\frac{1}{2}$ in. long, for the stakes. These are placed into position and worked with pairing in exactly the same way as the round base, until the lid is 4 in. in diameter. At this stage a bye-stake, $4\frac{1}{4}$ in. long, is inserted by the side of each of the stakes, and then the pairing is continued, using each bye-stake and stake separately, making forty stakes altogether. Let the lid be slightly arched like the base or it will not fit closely on the ledge of the basket, and will soon become twisted if it is made quite flat.

When the lid measures 7 in. across, work $\frac{1}{2}$ in. of pairing in coloured cane and then continue with the ordinary cane until the lid measures 9 in. To strengthen the edge of the lid before bordering, work two rows of waling, which will complete the necessary 9½ in. Carefully examine the lid to see that it is quite round and cut off all the stakes close to the work.

BORDER. No. 3 cane is used and a 6 in. piece must be pointed and inserted as far into the lid as possible by the side of each of the stakes. A three-rod plain border, Fig. 34, is then worked with these.

A small twisted ring (see handle, Fig. 74) should be made and fastened to the centre of the lid for lifting purposes.

SHALLOW SHOPPING BASKET (Fig. 99)

Materials required: 1 oz. No. 12 cane for base stakes; 6 oz. No. 9 cane for side stakes; 6 oz. No. 3 cane for weaving; 1 pair of handle canes; 2 pieces 5 mm. cane 10 in. long; 1 oz. wrapping cane.

This has a cane base 5 in. in diameter, which is made as described for the barrel-shaped basket, page 100; forty-one stakes 15 in. long of No. 9 cane are required for the sides, and when these have been inserted one row of pairing must be worked, as previously described, to cover the ends of the bottom stakes. The stakes do not require to be squeezed with the pliers for turning up at an acute angle as in some shaped baskets, but left as they are, straight out from the edge of the base to give the shallow shape illustrated. Work one row of four-rod upsetting as required at the beginning of the sides of all baskets with a cane base, and then two rows of three-rod upsetting, using No. 3 cane. The most convenient way to make this shaped basket, as already described, is to use a workboard resting on the knees and floor, as the work could not be seen well enough if on the table workboard. Peg the base down on to the board and shape all the stakes, bending each one a little more than necessary, as they will be inclined to straighten out during the working. Start randing with No. 3 cane in the ordinary way, taking care to get the shape correct and even. Work to a depth of 4 in., when the inside diameter should be about 10 in. Four rows of waling are then added before bordering. A three-rod plain border with follow-on trac is used, Fig. 59, page 60.

Fig. 99. RECTANGULAR SHOPPING BASKET WITH ROUNDED CORNERS
AND SHALLOW SHOPPING BASKET

HANDLE. Two canes are required, 8 mm. in thickness (about the size of a lead pencil). These, after being well shaped and pointed are inserted well down the basket. Three or four ¾ in. thin wire nails are useful to keep the canes together during the binding. The semicircular 5 mm. canes are inserted to further connect the handle to the basket. These are secured with a small nail where they touch the handle and included in the wrapping of the handle, as shown in the illustration, and as further described on page 65, Fig. 67.

RECTANGULAR SHOPPING BASKET WITH ROUNDED CORNERS (Fig. 99)

Materials required: 3 oz. No. 12 cane for base stakes; 3 oz. No. 3 cane for weaving base; 4 oz. No. 6 cane for side stakes; 4 oz. No. 2 cane for randing; ½ oz. No. 3 dyed cane for waling; 2 pieces 8 mm. cane 24 in. long for handle; ½ oz. pulp wrapping cane for handle; ½ oz. No. 4 cane for upsetting and waling.

Although oblong in shape when finished, this basket is commenced with an oval base, and therefore needs special attention as regards shaping during its progress.

For the working of the oval base, which measures 8¾ in. by 6¾ in. when complete, see page 101. Here cut eleven No. 12 canes 7½ in. long and seven 9½ in. long for the stakes. Make the space between the two groups of three short canes $2\frac{3}{4}$ in., with the remaining five canes spaced equally between them.

When the base is complete, cut sufficient stakes of No. 6 cane 14 in. long to insert in the base for the sides of the basket, one on each side of each stake round the ends of the base and also along each side, except in three places where a stake is inserted on one side of the base stakes only, to avoid making them too close together.

The stakes are used singly. Work one row of four-rod up-setting and three rows of three-rod upsetting with No. 4 cane, shaping the stakes well out to obtain the curved lower part of the basket. Next work three inches of randing with No. 2 cane, still paying attention to the shaping, and then one row of No. 3 dyed cane waling. Continue with two rows of double chain pairing (page 41) with No. 4 cane, and one more row of the dyed cane. Then do nine rows of randing with No. 2 cane and two rows of waling with No. 4 cane before bordering with a three-rod plain border and follow-on trac (Fig. 59, page 60). Aim at making the corners round and the sides and ends of the basket straight.

The handle is a variation of Fig. 68, page 66, being wrapped entirely. It is flat across the top, along which three canes are placed, two coloured and one cream, and in the wrapping the cane is taken under and over these alternately.

OBLONG SHOPPING BASKET (Fig. 101)

Materials required: 2 pieces of 8 mm. cane $11\frac{1}{2}$ in. long and 8 pieces of 5 mm. cane $11\frac{1}{2}$ in. long for base sticks; 4 oz. No. 5 cane for weaving base and for upsetting; 8 oz. No. 8 cane for side stakes of basket; 4 oz. No. 4 cane for weaving sides; 1 oz. No. 6 cane; 3 lengths enamelled cane; three pieces 8 mm. cane 26 in. long for handle, six pieces 8 in. long for temporary use in inserting handle.

OBLONG BASE. The working of an oblong base is quite different from a round or oval one, and can only be made by using a screwblock. This consists of two wooden blocks with thumb-screws for tightening purposes (see Fig. 100) and acts as a vice for holding the sticks (the name given to the stakes of an oblong

Fig. 100. OBLONG CANE BASE

base) in an upright position while the weaving is worked horizontally to and fro.

To work the base, first shave one end of each of the base sticks ready for inserting in the screw block as follows. Loosen the thumbscrews and place one 8 mm. cane and one 5 mm. cane close together near one end of the screwblock so that they measure $10\frac{1}{2}$ in. high above the block, and place another similar pair of canes further along the block to make a total width of $6\frac{1}{4}$ in. These canes form the outside sticks (sometimes called 'outsiders') of the base. Place the remaining six 5 mm. canes in the block in a similar manner between the outsiders, spacing them equally apart. (Only five are shown in Fig. 100.) Tighten the thumbscrews so that the canes are held firmly in an upright position for the weaving.

One row of pairing is worked at the beginning and ending of the base to strengthen the edges. The remainder is worked with randing. Bend a length of No. 5 cane to make two canes and work one row of pairing, after which secure one of the ends by threading it along two or three stakes and cut it off, as only one cane is required for the randing. This is worked from left to right in the ordinary way, turning the screwblock round after each row. The reversing is only suggested to simplify the working for the beginner. The experienced worker always works from left to right and from right to left alternately, without changing the position of the block. Care must be taken during the weaving to keep the sticks quite upright and the weaving level. To make the latter possible, the weaving cane must be wrapped entirely round the two outer canes at regular intervals, i.e. at either end of each alternate row. Further, the weaving should be tapped with the rapping iron. Keep all ends caused by joining on one side of the base, which will then be used for the underside. When a depth of $10\frac{1}{4}$ in. is reached, add a length of cane and work one row of pairing and secure the ends. This completes the weaving; the block is unscrewed and the base taken out. Cut off all ends to make the surface even and then cut off the ends of the six inside sticks quite close to the working.

SIDES. When the base is complete, lay it flat on a table with the best side uppermost, ready for inserting the stakes. Use a bodkin to make way for the stakes, first dipping it into a bar of soap, as this enables it to pass through the cane more easily.

Cut 112 stakes of No. 8 cane 15 in. long; i.e. seventeen stakes and bye-stakes for each side of the basket, and eleven stakes and bye-stakes for each end, and point the stakes ready for inserting. Beginning with the ends of the base, make a hole with the bodkin in the outside stick on either side of the base and insert the remaining stakes into the base as far as possible at equal distances apart, each time using the bodkin.

To insert the side stakes, first mark $\frac{1}{4}$ in. from either end of the base for the corner stakes and then equally divide the space between for the remaining fifteen stakes. Make a hole with the bodkin at the points marked through the outer pair of sticks and insert the stakes through the sticks and $\frac{1}{4}$ in. beyond, sloping upwards a little to make them secure. These protruding ends are afterwards cut off level with the work. The stakes are now squeezed in the usual way with round-nosed pliers, and bent up to form the sides.

Fig. 101. OBLONG SHOPPING BASKET

To begin weaving the sides of the basket, work one row of four-rod upsetting with two long pieces of cane squeezed in the middle and placed at the back of two stakes, to make the four necessary canes. At the end of the row, when the pattern has been completed, leave off one of the canes and continue with three-rod upsetting for another three rows. After working the first two rows place the base on a workboard, making sure that it is kept quite flat and that the stakes are placed at a slight angle and not upright. When the upsetting is completed add a bye-stake to of the stakes. Keep the two double stakes at each corner fairly close together and the sides and ends flat so that the basket does not lose its rectangular shape.

Work $2\frac{1}{2}$ in. of randing with No. 4 cane, then two rows of waling with No. 6 cane. After this add three rows of enamelled cane and two rows of No. 4 cane worked alternately, and then two more rows of waling with No. 6 cane.

Before working the border, which is a trac border, point the ends of the six 8 in. pieces of 8 mm. cane and insert them at

three points on each side of the basket where the handle is to
be placed. In working the border bend down the first pair of
stakes about 1½ in. deep and work it in front of two stakes,
behind one, in front of two, behind one, in front of one, leaving
the ends inside. Repeat in this manner and complete the border
as described in the trac borders on page 48.

When the border is complete the handle canes are bent into
shape and pointed at the ends. This being done, the six short
pieces of cane are removed and the handle canes inserted in their
places. These are nailed together across the centre for about 9 in.

To wrap the handle start at the middle with a length of pulp
wrapping cane, beginning with the middle of this also. Three
lengths of enamelled cane are placed along the top of the handle
and the pulp wrapping cane wrapped under and over them
alternately. These are cut off where the three handle canes diverge.
The wrapping is completed down one of the side handle canes
to the border and across over the front and back of it and the
end securely tucked away.

To wrap the other side piece of the handle a new piece of
wrapping cane must be introduced, taking it along the underside, after which the wrapping is continued as before. One half
of the handle being completed, the other half is repeated similarly
by starting at the centre again. Where a new length of cane is
required the join is made on the underside of the handle. Finally
the handle must be pegged with short pieces of No. 9 cane under
the two top rows of waling, as described on page 64 (a). It is
only necessary to peg two of the three handle canes on each side
of the basket.

LUNCHEON BASKET (Fig. 102)

Materials required: 8 pieces of 8 mm. cane 15 in. long, and 34
pieces of 5 mm. 15 in. long for base and lid; 1 piece of 8 mm.
30 in. long for handle and fastener; 8 oz. No. 4 for randing
sides; 8 oz. No. 5 for waling and weaving lid and base; 6 oz.
No. 9 for stakes, 14 in. long; 3 yds. No. 3 glossy seating cane
for wrapping handle.

The base measures 13 in. by 9 in. when complete, and here
again the same instruction applies for making it as described on

page 111. The sticks for the base are placed in the screwblock as follows: one pair of 8 mm. canes for each of the outside stakes with eight pairs of 5 mm. canes for the inside sticks placed between them at equal distances apart. The weaving is done with No. 5 cane.

When the base is complete the stakes for the side and ends of the basket are inserted as described in the previous basket. Here there are twenty-one stakes for each side and fifteen stakes for each end. Begin weaving at one end with No. 5 cane, looping a length of cane round two stakes to make four canes for working a row of four-rod upsetting. At the end of the row leave one cane off and continue with the remaining three canes for three rows of three-rod upsetting. The corner stakes must be kept fairly close together, and before starting to rand with No. 4 cane the two stakes at each corner are strengthened by adding a bye-stake to each one. Each pair of canes is worked as one in the weaving. This not only simplifies the working of the corners but makes them firmer.

Fig. 102. LUNCHEON BASKET

Work 3 in. of randing and four rows of waling with No. 5 cane, keeping the sides and corners upright. Before working the border, which is a four-rod plain border, see page 51, cut off the corner bye-stakes level with the last row of waling.

In the working of the basket care must be taken to keep the base always flat on the workboard. Should it become twisted, take it off the board and twist it back again into its right shape.

The top of the basket should measure approximately 14 in. by $10\frac{1}{2}$ in. when complete.

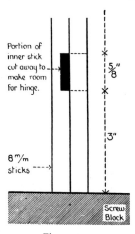

Portion of inner stick cut away to make room for hinge.

$\frac{5}{8}$"

3"

8 ⁿ/m sticks

Screw Block

Fig. 103

In making the lid set the sticks in the block $10\frac{1}{4}$ in. wide and $14\frac{1}{4}$ in. high, using double 8 mm. canes for the outsiders as in the base, and nine double 5 mm. canes spaced equally between them. Measure up and mark on the right-hand side pair of 8 mm. canes 3 in., then $\frac{5}{8}$ in., $6\frac{3}{8}$ in., $\frac{5}{8}$ in., 3 in. The last measurement is the length of the lid before bordering. The two $\frac{5}{8}$ in. spaces mark the position for the hinges. To make a space for inserting these, approximately half the width of the inner 8 mm. cane is cut away at these points (see Fig. 103). The randing is taken round the remaining half of the cane, leaving the outer cane uncovered so that the hinges will work freely.

In weaving the lid, begin and end with one row of pairing. Leave all the ends of the outside 8 mm. canes on until the border is worked at the ends of the lid, but cut off the 5 mm. canes close to the weaving.

A three-rod plain border, Fig. 34, page 50, is used with No. 9 cane.

BORDER. Cut stakes for working the border 8 in. long of No. 9 cane, and insert them on the left-hand side of the lid stakes with the best side of the lid towards the worker. Place a piece of No. 9 cane round the left-hand outside sticks of the lid (see Fig. 104). making the end marked E protrude about 3 in. and the other

H

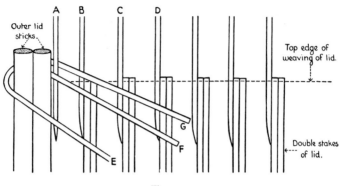

Fig. 104

end marked G 4 in. Insert the cane marked F between the cane G and the inner cane of the outsiders, making it protrude about 4 in. Then insert an additional stake, marked A, close to the outsider. Place E in front of A and behind B; bend down A at the back and by the side of E; next take F in front of B and behind C; bend down B at the back of F. Now take G in front of C and behind D and bend down C at the back of it. This will make three pairs of canes. Take the fifth cane each time in front of the left-hand cane that is standing upright and behind the next. Bend down the left-hand upright cane, and so on, until the right-hand side of the lid is reached. All the canes must be squeezed with the round-nosed pliers before bending down, as usual in bordering. When the last two canes worked are resting against the inner cane of the right-hand outsiders, place the next cane, which in its proper order is the fifth, in front of the last stake standing. Leave the end at the back. Now bend down the last stake behind the outsiders, round the front, and insert it by the right-hand of the pair of canes. Cut off all ends neatly and bind the beginning and finishing of the border with a soft piece of twisted No. 4 cane. Secure the ends by threading them away in the weaving.

The other end of the lid must be treated in the same way.

Now trim off all the ends of the outsiders in a slanting direction quite close to the border.

HINGES. To hinge the lid to the basket take a piece of No. 5

cane about 12 in. long, not too soft but not hard or brittle. Place the lid on the basket and mark the position of the hinges on the side of the basket. Insert the end of the cane down by the side of a stake at the position marked and twist the cane to make it flexible. After placing the lid again in position wrap round the space left on the outsiders and under the border approximately five times, securing the end of cane by threading it away.

It will be found helpful if, after the cane is twisted, a piece of soap is rubbed up and down it, as this makes the hinges work more freely.

Copper wire is sometimes used in place of cane for the hinges as it is stronger for this purpose.

THE FRONT FASTENINGS. The loops on the front side of the basket, through which the rod is passed, are made first. Loop a piece of fairly soft No. 9 cane round the sixth stake from the end of the basket and under the waling. Twist the two canes evenly and then twist them together tightly in the manner of a cord. Bend them over to make a loop with a space of $\frac{1}{2}$ in. inside and insert the ends one on either side of the stake $\frac{1}{2}$ in. below. Cross them over at the back and thread the ends away in the weaving.

Make the second loop in exactly the same way.

Now close down the lid and make a mark on the edge in line with the loops just made. Select two pieces of No. 9 cane 28 in. long, squeeze them with the pliers in the centre and point the ends. Make two holes with a bodkin (first dipped into a bar of soap) down between the two outsiders of the lid $\frac{3}{4}$ in. on each side of the mark just made. Thread one of the No. 9 canes through the first hole, twist the ends of cane and then twist them together for $4\frac{1}{2}$ in. Make a loop with this about $\frac{3}{4}$ in. deep and pass the two ends of cane round the double twist to secure the loop before continuing with the remainder of the double twist. When complete, thread the two ends of cane through the second hole, one from above and the other from underneath the lid, and secure by threading them along the lid. Make a second loop as described at the other end of the basket.

The sliding rod required for fastening is made of 8 mm. cane and should be about 12 in. long when complete, so that sufficient cane must be allowed for a loop at the end. This is shaped by first warming the cane in a gas jet or bunsen burner, being careful not to keep it in the flame too long or it will burn. The cane at the end of the loop is tapered off on the inside to fit alongside the cane and is secured by a ½-in. nail. It is then wrapped with narrow chair-seating cane. The other end of the rod is pointed a little.

HANDLE. The handle, which is round at the front and flat at the back, should measure 4 in. across the back and 2 in. from back to front, and is made of 8 mm. cane, being shaped over a flame as before, and then squeezed with the pliers to give sharply bent corners and a flat back. The two ends of the cane are spliced together in the middle of the back and secured with ½-in. nails.

The handle is wrapped with narrow chair-seating cane and is fastened on to the side of the basket with two twisted loops made as previously described for holding the rod.

POUCH-SHAPED SHOPPING BASKET WITH WRAPPED EDGE (Fig. 105)

SIZE OF BASKET, 10 IN. WIDE, 7½ IN. AT OPENING

Materials required: ½ oz. No. 12 cane for base stakes; 5 oz. No. 6 for side stakes; 5 oz. No. 1 cane for weaving; 2 pieces of 5 mm., 28 in. long, for rim; 1 piece 26 in. long, and 2 pieces 32 in. long, of 5 mm. for handle; ½ oz. No. 4 chair seating cane for wrapping; 4 lengths of black narrow enamelled cane; a few ⅜ in. and ½ in. wire nails; a cane base, 5 in. diameter, as described on page 100.

Sixty stakes of No. 6 cane, 12 in. long, are pointed and inserted well into the base, one on either side of the stake, and also one in the centre of the stake, making three stakes for each base stake. Work one row of pairing in front and behind these stakes to make the weaving level with the ends of the base stakes. No. 1 cane is used throughout for the weaving.

Continue pairing for three rows, using the single stakes and spacing them equally ready for the upsetting, which is done in the following manner. (As the shape is required to be rounded, the stakes must not be squeezed with the round-nosed pliers, as in other baskets.) Get three lengths of No. 1 cane and squeeze with the pliers. Bend them in half and place each loop behind alternate stakes (the hollow base being on the underside). Now

Fig. 105. POUCH-SHAPED SHOPPING BASKET

before starting the upsetting, place a piece of No. 6 cane on top of the six lengths of canes to form a core of the upset. Work the canes in front of five stakes and behind one, and under the core cane, and repeat. Just before the completion of the row, thin down the ends of the core cane to make a neat join, and draw through all the upsetting canes. This makes a bold and firm ridge for the basket to stand on.

Next work four rows of three-rod upsetting, and then shape all the stakes carefully. A better result can be obtained if three or four are bent at the same time.

Before starting the randing, it will be an advantage if a ring is made of twisted cane of No. 12 size and about 7 in. in diameter, and all the stakes put inside this to hold them together. Great care must be taken in randing and shaping the sides.

It might be mentioned that a basket of this kind should not be attempted until the simpler shapes have been done.

It must now be pegged down on to a workboard and held between the knees to get a better view of the shape during the working. Work to a depth of $5\frac{1}{2}$ in. and then work one row of waling. Finish off the ends and start the second row, but instead of over and behind the stake, take the left-hand cane under the other two and behind the stake (see page 41).

The introduction of the enamelled cane is worked as randing —first row enamelled cane, and finish off the end; next row, round cane on alternate stakes, and so on, until three rows of enamelled cane are worked with the two rows of round cane between. At this stage, or perhaps a little before, the cane ring could be dispensed with, as the stakes will have been set.

Now work six rows of chain waling, the same way as the two rows under the pattern work. Be sure that the waling is quite level. Then cut off every other stake level with the top of the waling, and squeeze the stakes that are left with pliers so that there is a space of $\frac{1}{8}$ in. under the cane when it is bent down. This must be squeezed again at the place where it touches the next upright stake, pointed about $\frac{3}{4}$ in. long and tucked down by the side of the stake. Each of the stakes must be treated in the same way.

The basket is now ready for the rim, and this is described on page 60. Note that in this instance 5 mm. cane is used and not 8 mm.

Now comes the handle which must be shaped so that the lines correspond with the sides of the basket. Decide on the height of the handle, point and insert the centre cane in its proper place and nail through the outer cane into the handle. It will be seen from the illustration that there are canes bent on either side of the centre cane. These must be nicely shaped and nailed in position, the part that touches the rim being thinned down.

In wrapping the rim, be sure to get the wrapping cane quite close together. Keep the cane damp all the time.

To wrap the handle, see page 64, Fig. 66.

OVAL SHOPPING BASKET WITH PLAITED BORDER WORKED ON THE SIDE (Fig. 106)

Materials required: 1 oz. No. 12 cane for base stakes: 6 oz. No. 7 cane for side stakes; 6 oz. No. 3 cane for weaving; 2 oz. No. 3

Fig. 106. OVAL SHOPPING BASKET WITH PLAITED BORDER ON SIDE

dyed cane for weaving; 1 oz. pulp wrapping cane; 2 pieces 36 in.
long, of 8 mm. cane for handle; oval base, size 10½ in. by 6 in.

Cut 5 pieces of No. 12 cane, 11½ in. long, and 12 pieces 7 in.
long. Split the 12 pieces one at a time for about 1 in. in the
centre. Insert one of the 11½ in. pieces. Slip on each in turn the
12 pieces 7 in. long, and then slide through the other four long
pieces and arrange the short ones so that there are two groups
of three 5½ in. apart and about 3 in. from the ends of the cane.
Now arrange equally the other six pieces singly.

For instructions for working the base, see pages 100-101.
Sixty-four stakes are required, 22 in. long, inserting one on
either side of the base stakes, except the two middle short base
stakes. These must have only one stake for each, as otherwise
the stakes in the sides would be much too close.

Squeeze all the stakes and work the four-rod upsetting as described on page 41. Shape the stakes and hold in position while working. Rand to a depth of $3\frac{1}{4}$ in. above the upset and work two rows of waling.

The block pattern is worked with pairing—dyed cane and natural—in groups of five rows. When the last of the five rows has been worked, finish the ends off and start again for the next group of five, but start the colour over the natural cane and the natural cane over the colour. Complete this second group and commence and complete the third group. After this four rows of waling are worked.

Before starting the border, wet the stakes well and allow to rest a few minutes. In this case the stakes are not squeezed with the pliers but bent down with a fairly small bend, not at all sharp. Bend in front of two stakes, behind one, and leave the ends outside. After this part of the border is complete, squeeze all the stakes at the place where they are resting against another stake.

The plaited border is done exactly as for a tray (see page 56), but, of course, in this case it is flat on the sides.

It might be mentioned that it is advisable before starting the first part of the border to insert in position four pieces of handle-size cane, so that when the basket is ready for the handle these can be removed and the handle canes put in their place. Besides securing the handle by piercing and threading through the wrapping cane, the two No. 3 canes that were used alongside of the dyed cane when wrapping the handle can be made use of to give extra security by inserting down the four rows of waling and threading the ends along the side over a stake or two. See pages 64-66 for suitable handles, and instructions for wrapping.

CHAPTER IX

HOW TO LINE VARIOUS CANE WORK BASKETS
(WITH DETAILS FOR MAKING THE BASKETS)

Some suggestions and instructions are given below for the benefit of workers who may wish to line the work-baskets described on page 138 and shown in Fig. 107 (page 122).

CHOICE OF MATERIAL

It is important that the right kind of lining be used, i.e. suitable for the purpose in quality, texture and colour. Avoid the cheap satins and tawdry materials one so often sees in baskets, for apart from the fact that they will not wear, they look anything but 'workmanlike' and suggest something to be looked at rather than something to be used. The material need not be expensive, and it is much better to use a good cotton material than a poor silk. There are attractive cotton materials to be had in gay stripes, checks or floral designs which make excellent linings. Those with small patterns are the most suitable, as they are more in harmony with the size of the baskets than larger patterns.

If a silk is used, choose a fairly heavy one, particularly if the basket happens to be a large one.

Consider the colour of the lining carefully. If there is any colour introduced in the basket, let the lining be chosen to tone with it. Use bright colours if possible: it makes one feel much more 'workish' to look at a gay lining than a dull one. Remember also that cane is light in colour and has a dull surface, so that materials with a background of the same colour should be avoided or the result will be uninteresting. If a plain colour is used, decorate it with a little embroidery: it will give it a distinctive and attractive appearance.

METHOD OF LINING

In many of the cheaper baskets bought ready lined it will be found that the linings are stuck in with glue on a cardboard

Fig. 107. LINED WORK BASKETS

foundation. This is done for speed, and fairly good results can
be obtained by the expert, but for the amateur it is a messy
process and less satisfactory than sewing the lining in the basket.
The latter method, therefore, is recommended unless for any
reason it is not practical, e.g. when there is no convenient place
to which the lining can be sewn securely. This, however, does
not occur very often.

A little padding is usually necessary for practical purposes, but it must not be overdone. In some of the padded work baskets one sees, the lining seems to be made up of a series of ugly bumps which provide numerous little crevices for collecting dust.

MATERIALS REQUIRED

CARDBOARD for the bottom and lid. This should be fairly stiff so that it does not bend while being covered with the lining.
WADDING, for padding the lining.
TACKING COTTON, for holding the wadding to the cardboard lid and bottom.
THREAD. Fairly thick strong thread similar in colour to the basket.
NEEDLES. Strong needles, fairly coarse, for using with the thread to sew in the lining, and ordinary sewing and embroidery needles.
LINING MATERIAL and a reel of silk or cotton to match it.
EMBROIDERY SILKS and small wooden BEADS for decorative purposes and for securing or 'studding' the padding to the lid.
CORD for drawing up a 'pouch' lining.

WORKING INSTRUCTIONS

The arrangement of the lining can be varied according to the type of basket to be lined, and also to suit the particular taste of the worker. The simplicity of the process of lining depends largely on the order in which the various steps are carried out, so that this should be noted in the description of the following baskets which show a few of the many ways of arranging the lining.

No. 1 LINING

This basket, which has a cane base, is very simply lined. The pad for the bottom is made first, then the side pieces cut out and sewn in, and after this the pad is sewn in.
BASE. Measure the diameter of the bottom of the basket first, either with a tape measure or a pair of compasses. Special care should be taken to get it exact, for a base which is too small or too large is not easy to sew in, so that if it does not fit at first, persevere until it is correct. Draw with the compasses a circle the size required on some fairly stiff cardboard and cut it out,

then, as in most baskets with a cane base the base is slightly raised at the centre, cut a hole in the centre of the cardboard so that only a ring remains as shown in Fig. 108, Diag. 1. This allows it to lie flat in the bottom of the basket.

Now add the padding, and afterwards cover it with the material. Fold a sheet of wadding to make two thicknesses, place the ring on this and cut round the edge, then hold the wadding in position on the cardboard wind over and over it with tacking cotton (see Diag. 2), taking care to keep the edge of the wadding level with that of the cardboard. When this has been done, place the pad face downwards on the wrong side of the lining material and cut round it, leaving a $1\frac{1}{2}$ in. margin beyond. Then with a needle and thread gather round the edge of the material about $\frac{1}{2}$ in. in, starting and finishing on the right side of the material. Place the pad face downwards in the centre of the wrong side of the material, take both ends of the gathering thread, draw them up and tie them firmly together. Then to hold the material firmly in position on the pad, lace the edges together on the underside with thread, as shown in Diag. 3.

SIDE. Now that the pad for the bottom is completed, cut a strip of the lining material for the side of the basket. For the size measure the circumference of the inside of the top of the basket and add about 2 in. for joining purposes, then measure the depth of the side of the basket from under the border and add 2 in. to this for turning under at the top edge and for going under the pad at the lower edge.

SEWING THE LINING INTO THE BASKET. The same method of 'sewing in' is used in all the baskets shown, so that it is not necessary to describe it in detail more than once.

The sewing is carried from right to left.

Turn down the top edges of the side piece of material, place this immediately below the border of the basket and hold it in position with the left hand. Thread a needle with thread and pass it through the material between the border and the top row of the weaving of the basket to the outside, then pass the thread round one of the upright stakes of the basket and bring it back

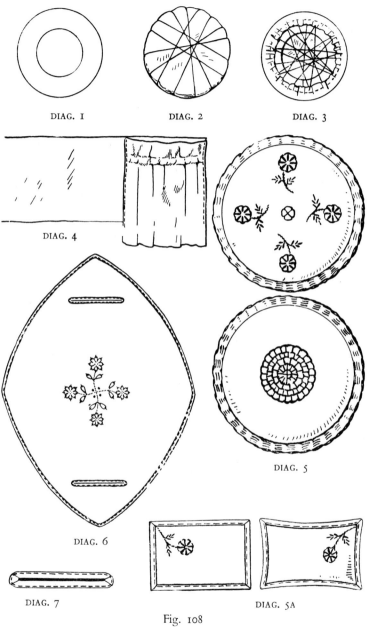

DIAG. 1   DIAG. 2   DIAG. 3

DIAG. 4

DIAG. 6

DIAG. 5

DIAG. 7   DIAG. 5A

Fig. 108

between the border and the top row of weaving, through the material. Pass along on the inside in front of one stake and then through again to the outside just before another stake, round this and back to the inside of the basket, and so on. If the thread is pulled fairly tightly the stitches will be hidden amongst the cane on the outside and under the border on the inside. A narrow cord can be added later, however, if necessary. Care must be taken not to pass the needle *through* any of the canes, or the stitches will show.

When the starting-point is almost reached, turn the end of the remaining piece under for about $\frac{1}{2}$ in. before sewing it in. This will wrap over the first end for a short distance. Crease this edge down with the fingers and slip stitch it to the first end with cotton or silk.

Now gather along the lower edge of the material with thread, leaving the end of thread hanging. Regulate the gathers and arrange the lining to the side of the basket ready for fitting in and sewing in the bottom pad. Place this in position and insert one or two pins through it to the basket to hold during the sewing in. Thread is used again. Bring the needle up from the underside of the basket, arranging so that the needle will pick up a small piece of the material at the edge of the pad while doing so, then take it down again through the basket immediately below, but not through the material of the pad this time. Pass the thread round a stake or, if the stakes are in groups, round one group of stakes of the base and up again as before, picking up a piece of material at the edge of the pad, and so on. Care must be taken to see that the pad is kept carefully in position, or it may be found towards the end that the edge of the pad appears to be too large for the basket. When the starting-point is reached fasten off the end of thread securely, and the main part of the lining will be completed. Next sew a narrow cord under the top rim if necessary, to hide any stitches, as already mentioned.

Should it be desirable to put a pincushion and needle-book into the basket, they can be made in the following manner:

PINCUSHION. A small piece of some firm material through which pins and needles can be easily passed is required for an interlining. Cut out two rectangular pieces of the basket-lining material, 4 in. by 2¾ in., with a piece of the interlining of the same size for each. Place these together with the interlined sides touching, and machine round the two sides and bottom edges, then fill this with bran or wadding and tack and machine the top edges together.

When this has been done bind the edges with narrow ribbon about ½ in. wide to tone with the lining, or a narrow strip of the material, sewing it on with running stitches of embroidery silk (see Diag. 5A).

NEEDLE-BOOK. This is made in a similar manner to the pin-cushion. In this case the pieces are machined together round the entire edge to make a flap piece. When this has been done cut two pieces of flannel a little smaller in size, gimp the edges and oversew the flannel to the underside of the flap piece along the top edge; then bind the edges with ribbon to correspond with the pincushion.

The pincushion and needle-book can now be sewn into the basket. They are sewn just below the border; one of them can be placed over the join of the material and the other immediately opposite to it. It is only necessary to secure them at the two top corners of each.

No. 2 LINING

This basket is similar in shape to the previous one, but has a wooden base. The sides of the lining are padded a little. The order of lining is the same as before.

Measure the size of the base first, cut it out in cardboard, but this time the hole need not be cut at the centre, as the base is quite flat. Cover the cardboard with wadding and material as before. Now cut a strip of material for the side of the basket, taking the measurements as before. A pocket is added to this before it is sewn. Cut out a piece of material for the pocket; the size, of course, will vary according to the size of the basket. If the basket measures about 4 in. deep below the border rim, then the pocket is cut about 6½ in. wide by 7 in. deep. This depth will allow for a 1¼ in. hem or heading at the top of the pocket and sufficient material to go under the pad and pouch a little at the bottom.

When the pocket has been cut out, turn down the top hem on to the wrong side and machine along the lower edge and then again about $\frac{1}{4}$ in. above this, to make a slot for a piece of narrow elastic. Thread the elastic in and draw the pocket up until it measures $4\frac{1}{2}$ in. Sew the elastic at either end to secure it and then turn and press the side edges down for $\frac{1}{4}$ in.

Now turn down the top edge of the side strip of lining and also the right-hand end about $\frac{1}{4}$ in. Place the edge of the pocket here to the edge of the material and machine it on as shown in Diag. 4, page 129. The wadding for padding the side is cut out next. A strip of double thickness the exact depth of the side, and long enough to fit round it with the ends closely meeting, is required. Sew it in round the top edge just below the cane ledge on which the lid rests. The stitches on the inside can be fairly long ones, as they are only required to hold the wadding in position while sewing in the side piece.

When this has been done the side piece can be sewn in; the pocket end will be sewn in last and will wrap over the first end. The edge of the pocket is sewn down to this end over the machine stitches at the side of the pocket. The pocket is sewn to the basket next at either end of the elastic, so that it will not pull out of position when in use.

Now the lower edge is gathered ready for sewing in the base. Do not gather along the bottom edge of the pocket, but only the material behind it.

Place and pin the base in position and start sewing it in close to one edge of the pocket, inserting the needle each time just above the edge of the wooden base. Continue round the base as far as the other edge of the pocket, then before sewing the remaining portion put the hand inside the pocket and pouch it a little at the lower edge, taking care not to draw the under material up while doing so. Then proceed with the sewing-in to the starting-point.

THE LID. A pad is made for the cane lid in a similar manner to the base, but with four thicknesses of wadding instead of two. The pad should not extend right to the edge of the lid, as this would prevent the lid fitting into the basket properly. Leave a ½ in. margin, therefore, all round when taking the measurement for the size. When the pad is made, if the material is a plain one and could be improved with a little embroidery, this should be done next. Diag. 5 gives two suggestions, one in which four small sprays of flowers are worked and the other with a centre circular medallion of rows of button-holing in various colours. Before sewing in the lid, sew a small flat wooden bead in the centre of the pad through the cardboard to hold the lining tight so that it does not readily become loose in wear. Then sew the pad in, taking care to keep it in the centre of the lid, slanting the needle so that the stitches are hidden under the pad.

A needle-book and pincushion can be added if desired, although possibly with the padded lid this might not be necessary. If it is decided to add these they can be decorated in one corner with embroidery to correspond with the lid (see Diag. 5A).

No. 3 LINING

The lining of the actual basket is similar to the first one, but here a material lid is added. The basket has a small cane ledge like the No. 2 basket on which the lid can rest. Measure the diameter of the basket on this ledge to find the size of the lid, then cut this out from a stiff piece of cardboard. Both sides of the cardboard are padded. Pad one side first with two thicknesses of wadding, winding it with tacking cotton to hold it in position, then pad the other side in the same way. Cut out a piece of material 1½ in. larger all round than the pad, and cover one side of it in the same way as covering the pad for the base, but do not lace the edges together. Take care to see that the threads of the material are straight across the centre of the pad and not pulled out of position. Cut out another circle of material this time, only ½ in. larger than the pad, and cover the other side of the pad with this, turning the edges under and pinning them to the material of the other side at regular intervals, again taking care to get the material quite straight. Then, when the pinning is complete, oversew the edges together, and afterwards, to make the edge neat, bind it with ribbon, taking the stitches of embroidery silk backwards and forwards through the cardboard.

I

Here again, if plain material is used, add a little embroidery: it will make it so much more interesting.

For the purpose of lifting the lid, wind a bone or brass ring about the size of a penny with the same ribbon as used for the binding, securing the ends by tying them in a bow. Sew this in the centre of the top side of the lid, through the cardboard with the bow resting on the lid. Then at the same place on the under-side sew a flat wooden bead.

No. 4 LINING

All three work baskets previously described have been round ones; No. 4 shows a boat-shaped basket. While the lining is very similar, the method of obtaining the shape of the cardboard base is of necessity a little different, for, of course, it cannot be made with the compasses this time.

Take a piece of brown paper of medium stiffness and place it in the bottom of the basket, then with the fingers smooth it over the base and crease it carefully into the edges and corners and draw round it with a pencil so that the exact pattern of the base is obtained. When taking it out of the basket pencil an arrow on the paper, pointing towards one end of the basket, and another on the wooden base of the basket to correspond; this will ensure the base being put in the correct way, as the two ends of a basket sometimes vary a little. Cut the paper pattern out and then place it on a piece of stiff cardboard, carefully draw round it and cut the cardboard out, not forgetting to put the arrow on the under-side as on the paper. Try it in the basket, and if it seems a little too small in places mark these on the base with the pencil, or in the same way, if it is too large, mark it so that the pieces can be cut off. Probably with the beginner one or two bases will have to be cut before a good fit is obtained, but it is well worth while to persevere, as it makes such a difference to the success of the lining. Practice does much in this direction. It is quite simple a matter to remove the cardboard base from the basket if a bradawl or some similar implement is used from the outside of the basket to raise it up. This method of obtaining the pattern of the base can be used for a basket of any shape.

The cardboard is padded and covered in a similar manner to the round bases, being laced with thread from side to side and

end to end on the underside. The sides are padded like the No. 2
basket, but here there is a pocket at either end of the basket.
These are made and machined on as in the previous basket before
the side is sewn in. Sew one pocket on at the left-hand end of the
strip, place it in position in the basket and carefully measure the
side piece round the basket and mark the position of the other
pocket. This must be accurately done or it will be discovered too
late that the pocket is not where it ought to be.

When the wadding has been cut out and sewn in, place the
material in position in the basket, pinning the pockets in the centre
of either end, then start sewing it in, beginning immediately after
the first pocket so that the final end can be tucked under this
before the pocket is sewn down. When the sewing-in is completed, sew the edge of the pocket down to the underneath
material and then gather round the lower edge, omitting the edge
of the pockets as before. Although there are not any actual
gathers, as the sides are vertical, this helps to hold the material
down tightly. Place the material in position so that it fits to the
side and corners of the basket, adjusting the gathering as required,
and then insert the bottom pad. This should hold the sides down
tightly, and if they appear at all loose take the pad out, draw the
gathering thread up a little more and try again. When this has
been done satisfactorily sew the pad in, starting just beyond one
of the pockets. When the first pocket is reached pouch it at the
lower edge a little before proceeding with the sewing, and also
again at the second pocket. The line of stitches on the outside of
the basket should be immediately above the edge of the wooden
base as in basket No. 2.

This particular basket has only a narrow border edge, so that
in order to hide the sewing-in stitches at the top, a narrow cord
is sewn over them just below the border. A 'lacing' cord is
suitable. The colour should be chosen to tone with the lining or
be the colour of the basket. A needle-book and pincushion can
be added if desired in the centre of the two sides.

LID OR COVER. A material cover serves as a lid here. The
shape of this is shown in Diag. 6, page 129. It has four points
which are arranged to hang down the sides and ends of the

basket to approximately 1 in. from the base, so that measurements must be taken accordingly, for the size of the cover will depend upon the size of the basket.

When the distance between the two sets of points is determined mark this on a piece of paper and then join them up with a slightly curved line as shown, so that it will fit well over the corners of the basket. To get the four curves symmetrical, when one has been made, the paper can be folded through the points and all of them cut together. When the paper pattern has been made, cut the material out, then bind the edges with ribbon, taking care not to stretch them out of shape. The ribbon can be sewn on as before with a running stitch of embroidery silk.

To enable the cover to lie flat over the basket an opening or slit must be made for each of the handles. Measure accurately the distance between the handles for the position of the slits and the length of the handles for the length of the slits. Mark this on the cover and then extend the slits for $\frac{1}{4}$ in. at either end; this is to allow for binding. Then cut them and bind them with the ribbon, taking special care at the ends of the slits. Start about 1 in. from one of the ends, as it is easier to join here. When the binding is complete, the inner edge of the binding can be pleated over at each of the ends of the slits so that it lies flatter (see Diag. 7). Now that all the binding is complete, if the material is plain add a little embroidery in the centre of the cover as suggested in Diag. 6, and on the needle-book and pincushion to correspond; also to each of the four points of the cover sew one or two coloured wooden beads to help to weight and hold the cover in position on the basket.

NO. 5 LINING

This shows a very useful method of lining, namely, the pouch lining, which is almost like a bag. The inside of the basket is lined first up to the lower edge of the band of openwork, and then the pouch is added later, for in this way the right side of the material can be made to show in the inside of the basket and also through the openwork band. If desired, the inside lining can be of a different material; for example, natural tussore the colour of the basket looks very well and is serviceable. The inside lining is made and sewn in just the same way as the lining in No. 1 and No. 3 baskets, with one pocket.

The pouch is made as follows: Measure round the circumference of the basket on the inside, just below the top border edge, and add about 2 in. to this measurement to allow for turnings and the sewing-in (this amount is for a basket of 12 in. diameter: a little more would be necessary for a larger basket). Here the depth of the pouch is about 16 in. This allows for a 2 in. hem or heading at the top and sufficient material to reach to the lower edge of the openwork band (again for a larger basket a deeper pouch would be necessary). Cut out the material and seam up the two ends, then turn a 2 in. hem down on to the wrong side for the top of the pouch and machine it along the lower edge, and then again about $\frac{3}{4}$ in. above to make a slot for the cords which draw the pouch up. Then, to make openings for inserting the cord, work four buttonholes, two against the seam, one on either side of it, so that they are about 1 in. apart, and two others also 1 in. apart on either side of the corresponding centre point of the pouch immediately opposite the seam.

If the pouch is to be embroidered, it is most easily done before it is sewn into the basket. The position of the embroidery can be judged by placing the pouch to the side of the basket and marking with chalk where the top edge will come. The embroidery can take the form of a simple border, running round the pouch about 2 in. away from the top edge of the basket, or a series of small flower sprays or simple motifs placed at regular intervals.

The pouch is sewn in round the lower edge of the openwork border first.

Place the pouch upside down in the basket with the right side inside, and bring the bottom edge of the pouch to just below the open border. Sew it in the basket in this position about $\frac{1}{4}$ in. below the edge of the material, so that it can be turned up afterwards and sewn again at the top of the border underneath the top rim, and at the same time be quite neat on the right side with the right side of the material showing on the outside of the basket.

When the sewing-in is complete, the cords are threaded in the slot. An ordinary 'lacing' cord, of some colour to tone with the lining, is suitable. Two lengths are required, each one long enough to pass completely round the basket with an additional 6 in. for tying purposes. Start threading one cord through the buttonhole on one side of the seam and continue round the pouch and out again at the buttonhole on the other side of the seam, then thread the second cord in one of the other buttonholes, round the pouch and out of the second buttonhole.

Knot the two ends together in each case and cut the protruding ends quite close to the knot, then sew through each of the knots with cotton or silk to secure them and add one or two bright coloured wooden beads at the end of each.

NO. 6 LINING

This is the No. 1 basket shown in Fig. 107, but with a pouch lining.

TO MAKE WORK BASKETS IN FIG. 107

Nos. 1 and 6. ROUND BASKET WITH A CANE BASE
Materials required: 1 oz. No. 12 cane for base stakes; 6 oz. No. 6 cane for side stakes; 4 oz. No. 3 cane for weaving.

Cut ten stakes 7 in. long for the base, which is worked as described on page 97. Cut sufficient stakes to insert in the base for the side of the basket, making them 17 in. long. Work one row of pairing round the edge of the base as described, and then bend the stakes up sharply for the side of the basket. Work one row of four-rod upsetting and three rows of three-rod upsetting, placing the stakes at an angle of 45 degrees. Cut bye-stakes 6 in. long and insert them on the right of each stake. Work $\frac{1}{2}$ in. randing and one row of waling. Next mark the stakes for the band of fitching, Fig. 24, page 44. The rows are $\frac{3}{4}$ in. apart. Work four rows of waling above the last row. Cut off the bye-stakes close to the last row of waling and then proceed to work a two-rod five-stroke plaited border, page 55.

No. 2. WORK BASKET WITH LID has been described previously on page 103.

No. 3. ROUND WORK BASKET

Materials required: 1 oz. No. 12 cane for base stakes; 6 oz. No. 6 cane for side stakes; 4 oz. No. 3 cane for weaving.

This basket measures 10 in. in diameter at the top and 5 in. at the base. It is 4 in. deep with the sides sloping out at an angle of 45 degrees. It is very similar to the No. 1 basket. The base is worked in the same way and the sides begin in a like manner.

After the upsetting, the randing is continued to a depth of 2 in., after which two rows of waling are worked before adding the fitching. When this is complete two more rows of weaving are worked and a trac border, Fig. 31, using the double stakes and leaving the ends on the inside. These are used later to work a simple trac border, which serves as a ledge for the lid to rest upon, as in the No. 2 basket.

No. 4. WORK BASKET WITH BOWED SIDES

Materials required: Wooden base 16 in. by 9 in., the corner holes bored large enough to take 8 mm. cane handles; 6 oz. No. 8 cane for stakes; 8 oz. No. 3 cane for weaving; two pieces (18 in. long) of 8 mm. cane for handles; eight pieces (5 in. long) of split 8 mm. cane for inserting in the sides of the basket.

First shape the handle canes and insert them in the corner holes, allowing the ends to protrude $\frac{1}{2}$ in. below the base to serve as feet. Secure them by driving a $\frac{1}{2}$ in. nail through the edge of the base, cutting off the head before finally driving it in.

Insert the stakes, and work a foot border on the under side. Work two rows of three-rod upsetting on the top side and rand to a height of $2\frac{3}{4}$ in. above the base. Introduce two rows of waling and then continue to rand for 1 in., after which work two more rows of waling.

The eight pieces of split cane are inserted down the sides of the basket before working the border. These are arranged in pairs and threaded through the rows of waling where the cane passes in front of two stakes, counting about three stakes from the corner and leaving two stakes between each pair. They must be cut off flush with the top row of waling, after which a three-rod border with a follow-on trac, Fig. 59, is worked.

If preferred the handle canes and split canes can be coloured, or the handles wrapped with enamelled cane.

No. 5. BOWL-SHAPED WORK BASKET

Materials required: 1 oz. of No. 12 cane for base stakes; 4 oz. No. 9 cane for side stakes; 5 oz. No. 3 cane for weaving; 2 pieces of 8 mm. 38 in. long for the rim; 1 oz. of pulp wrapping cane and a few $\frac{3}{8}$ in. and $\frac{3}{4}$ in. nails.

The basket is 11 in. in diameter at the top and 4 in. deep.

When the base has been made in the manner described on page 100, cut the stakes for the side 8 in. long. When these have been inserted they are not squeezed and turned up as described, but left flat until later.

Work one row of four-rod upsetting, followed by three rows of three-rod upsetting. Now shape the stakes and place a ring of cane over them as mentioned in the hints on page 29.

Rand to a depth of 2 in. and add two rows of waling. Next insert a bye-stake on each side of the stakes in readiness for working the fitching, Fig. 23, page 43. Work two rows of waling above this and then proceed with the rim as described on page 61, Fig. 60.

SUGGESTED SCHEDULES

Suggested schedule of canework materials and tools required for one year for a class of 20 pupils aged 8-11.

40 round 7 in. bases for round teapot stands
40 square 7 in. bases for square teapot stands
40 round 3 in. bases for glassholders
40 round 6 in. bases for small work baskets
40 round 6 in. bases for small paper baskets
40 oval 9 in. by 5 in. bases for cake or roll baskets
2 lb. No. 1 pulp cane for weaving
20 lb. No. 2 pulp cane for weaving
5 lb. No. 3 pulp cane for weaving
10 lb. No. 4 pulp cane for weaving
14 lb. No. 5 pulp cane for weaving
2 lb. No. 3 dyed pulp cane for weaving
1 lb. pulp wrapping cane
6 pairs round-nosed pliers
4 pairs shears
10 small bodkins
20 bradawls
10 knives

Suggested schedule of canework materials and tools required for one year for a class of 20 pupils aged 11-14.

6 oval 18 in. by 10 in. bases for trays
6 oblong 18 in. by 10 in. bases for trays
6 round 14 in. bases for trays
40 round 8 in. bases for work baskets
40 oval 9 in. by 5 in. bases for cake or roll baskets
40 round 8 in. bases for paper baskets
13 lb. size 3 pulp cane for weaving
2 lb. pulp wrapping cane for weaving and wrapping
4 lb. size 3 dyed cane for weaving
25 lb. size 4 pulp cane for weaving
6 lb. size 5 pulp cane for stakes
45 lb. size 6 pulp cane for stakes
7 lb. size 9 pulp cane for stakes ⎫ (for bases of shopping
1 lb. size 12 pulp cane for stakes ⎭ baskets)
2 lb. 8 mm. cane for handles
4 dozen lengths enamelled cane, assorted colours
6 pairs round-nosed pliers
4 pairs shears
20 bradawls
10 knives
10 small bodkins
5 bent bodkins

Suggested schedule of canework materials and tools required for one year for a class of 20 pupils aged above 14 years.

> 6 oval 18 in. by 10 in. bases for trays
> 6 rectangular 18 in. by 10 in. bases for trays
> 6 round 14 in. bases for trays
> 20 round 8 in. bases for round work baskets
> 20 oval 9 in. by 5 in. bases for oval work baskets or bread baskets
> 20 round 8 in. bases for paper baskets
> 20 18 in. by 10 in. bases and partitions for knife baskets
> 20 bases for lemonade tray baskets,
> also sufficient materials for making 20 shopping baskets
> which are included below:
> 36 lb. No. 3 cane for weaving
> 20 lb. No. 4 cane for weaving
> 12 lb. No. 5 cane for stakes
> 15 lb. No. 6 cane for stakes
> 7 lb. No. 7 cane for stakes
> 7 lb. No. 8 cane for stakes
> 7 lb. No. 9 cane for stakes ⎫
> 1 lb. No. 12 cane for stakes ⎬ shopping baskets
> 3 lb. 8 mm. cane for handles ⎭
> 5 dozen assorted enamelled canes
> 4 lb. size 3 dyed cane
> 2 lb. pulp wrapping cane
> 10 pairs round-nosed pliers
> 6 pairs shears
> 20 bradawls
> 10 knives
> 10 small bodkins
> 5 bent bodkins.

SUGGESTIONS FOR THE CANEWORK COURSE

AN OUTLINE SCHEME FOR A FOUR-YEAR COURSE IN CANE BASKETRY

YEAR I: AGES 9 TO 10

Read and study the chapter on the history of basket-making in this book, and also the sections on the growth and preparation of cane and hints to the worker. Collect any photographs appertaining to cane and its uses.

Start the practical work by making the following articles:

Round and square teapot stands (Figs. A and B).
Glass holders (Fig. C)
Small work baskets (Fig. D, page 142)
Small paper baskets
Oval cake or roll baskets (Fig. E, page 142).

All the above to include the working of simple borders and the introduction of simple patterns in colour.

Materials required

Small bases of various sizes from 3 to 7 ins. Pulp cane Nos. 3 to 5, and some dyed cane and wrapping cane. An assortment of round and oval beads.

YEAR 2: AGES 10 TO 12

Larger articles should now be attempted, such as the following:

Oval and oblong trays (Figs. F and G).

Round and oval work baskets (Fig. H).

The trays should be worked with plain and plaited borders with pattern work of enamelled cane and coloured beads.

Trac borders and pattern work in dyed cane should be worked into the work baskets.

Materials required

Larger bases in assorted sizes, and pulp cane as for the first-year course are required. Some lengths of enamelled cane should be included.

YEAR 3: AGES 12 TO 14

The same type of work as for the second year is to be carried out, but with the addition of shopping baskets.

Trays of various shapes and sizes.

Work baskets: various kinds and with new weaving patterns (Figs. K, page 142, and J, 140).

New shapes in paper baskets.

Round shopping baskets.

Baskets with a cane base should be attempted, with colour introduced into sides and handle.

Materials required

Some thicker cane for staking larger articles and for the base stakes of baskets will be required, in addition to the usual supply of cane and bases as for previous years.

YEAR 4: OVER 14

The type of work now to be attempted will depend on how the pupils have progressed in the previous years. Certain advanced students may attempt work stands, small chairs, dinner waggons, etc., on frames. This is expensive, and for general school work the following scheme is recommended:

More complicated baskets with cane bases (round, oval and oblong)

(Figs. L, M and N).

Work baskets with cane bases.

Knife baskets (Fig. O).

Lemonade tray baskets.

SUGGESTIONS FOR THE CANEWORK COURSE

Materials required

A range of materials similar to the third year will be required.

Tools for the Course

With very slight modification, one set of tools will cover all four courses. The principal tools are round-nosed pliers, shears, bodkins, bradawls and knives.